D0762805

IF CHRIST CAME TO THE OLYMPICS

William J. Baker, Bird and Bird Professor of History at the University of Maine, received his BD (Divinity) degree from Southeastern Seminary in the United States, and his PhD from Cambridge University. He is the author or editor of eight books, including *Beyond Port and Prejudice: Charles Lloyd of Oxford, 1784–1829* (1981), *Sports in the Western World* (1982, 1988), *Jesse Owens: An American Life* (1986), and (with J.A. Mangan) *Sport in Africa: Essays in Social History* (1987).

NEW COLLEGE
LECTURES

IF CHRIST CAME TO THE OLYMPICS

William J. Baker

UNSW
PRESS

A UNSW Press book

Published by
University of New South Wales Press Ltd
UNSW SYDNEY NSW 2052
AUSTRALIA
www.unswpress.com.au

© New College 2000
First published 2000

This book is copyright. Apart from any fair dealing for the purpose of private study, research, criticism or review, as permitted under the Copyright Act, no part may be reproduced by any process without written permission. Inquiries should be addressed to the publisher.

National Library of Australia
Cataloguing-in-Publication entry:

Baker, William J. (William Joseph).
If Christ came to the Olympics.

ISBN 0 86840 579 5.

1. Olympics — Religious aspects. 2. Sports — Religious aspects. 3. Sports — Religious aspects — Christianity. I. Title. (Series: New College lecture series)

796.01

Printer Southwood Press
Cover photo Courtesy of Amateur Athletic Foundation

NEW COLLEGE
LECTURES
AND
PUBLICATIONS

New College is an Anglican college affiliated with the University of New South Wales, Sydney. In 1986 the college set up a trust to conduct an annual series of public lectures. The lecturer is asked to take up some aspect of contemporary society and to comment on it from the standpoint of their Christian faith and professional experience. The inaugural lectures were given in 1987 by Professor Malcolm Jeeves of St Andrews University, Scotland, and in subsequent years lecturers have come from Australian and overseas universities, as well as the wider community.

1987   Prof Malcolm Jeeves (University of St Andrews, Scotland)
       Minefields, Lancer Books (ANZEA), 1994.

1988   Dr Veronica Brady (University of Western Australia)
       Can These Bones Live? Federation Press, 1997.

1989   The Hon Keith Justice Mason (NSW Supreme Court)
       Constancy and Change, Federation Press, 1990.

1990   Prof Stanley Hauerwas (Duke University, USA)
       After Christendom?, ANZEA, 1991.

1991   Prof Geoffrey Bolton (University of Queensland).

1992   Prof Peter Newman (Murdoch University, Western Australia).

1993   Prof Robin Gill (University of Kent, England)
Beyond Self Interest, New College, 1993.

Rev Dr John Polkinghorne, KBE, FRS (Queens' College, Cambridge)
Religion and Current Science, New College, 1993.

1994   Prof Geoffrey Brennan (Australian National University).

1995   Rev Dr John Polkinghorne, KBE, FRS (Queens' College, Cambridge)
Beyond Science, Cambridge University Press, 1996; Polish ed, 1998; Greek ed, 1999.

1996   Les Murray (Australian poet)
Killing the Black Dog, Federation Press, 1997.

1997   Dr Elaine Storkey (London Institute for Contemporary Christianity, England)
Constructed or Created: The Great Gender Debate, Paternoster Press/UNSW Press, 2000

1998   Dr Peter Vardy (Heythrop College, University of London)
What Is Truth?, UNSW Press, 1999.

CONTENTS

FOREWORD

by Christine Alexander,
New College Lectureship Trust

On the eve of the Sydney Olympics, the question of ethics in sport could not be more relevant. An obsession to win at all costs reduces sport for many athletes and spectators alike to the pursuit of money, power and fame. The regular allegations about drug abuse, petulant athletes devoid of team spirit and the corruption of Olympic officials strongly suggest this.

Professor William Baker's lecture series 'If Christ came to the Sydney Olympics' was timely indeed. Delivered as the New College Lectures for 1999, the series has now been expanded in this book to include all Olympic occasions. Thus the book has the same provocative title, *If Christ Came to the Olympics*, questioning the conscience of the modern Olympic Movement in the face of rampant commercialism, reported bribing of officials, boycotts, demonstrations, politically-motivated violence and cheating with performance-enhancing drugs.

William Baker is Bird and Bird Professor of History at the University of Maine, USA, and an internationally recognised

X ● IF CHRIST CAME TO THE OLYMPICS

scholar in the history of sport and sport and religion. Born in Tennessee in 1938, he studied for his BA in history, English and philosophy at Furman University (1960) on a football scholarship. After an interlude at the University of Zurich, Switzerland, where he pursued his interest in theology, he studied for a Bachelor of Divinity at Southeastern Seminary in North Carolina, then a liberal Baptist seminary. He received his PhD from Cambridge University, UK, in 1967, with a dissertation on 'The Attitudes of English Churchmen, 1800–1850, Toward the Reformation'. Since 1970, Professor Baker has taught at the University of Maine, where he has been Chair of the Department of History since 1994. He also teaches church history part-time at the non-denominational Bangor Theological Seminary in Maine.

In the following pages, Professor Baker challenges us with an analogy between religion and sport, an idea that was not far from the mind of Baron Pierre de Coubertin when he first created the modern Olympic Movement in 1896 to be 'like religion but without the dogma'. To what extent are we simply 'going for gold' in our lives? Quoting the Protestant theologian Paul Tillich, Baker reminds us that one's 'ultimate concern' is one's religion, and that sport is perhaps the most dominant of all false gods in which people invest.

Each year the New College Lectures seek to make a useful contribution to Christian debate in Australian Society. The views expressed in this book may not necessarily be those of New College, and we may not all agree with Professor Baker's scepticism about what he calls 'prime time proselytising'. Few will disagree, however, with his call for a return to the ideals of the amateur, enshrined in the Olympic charter, where the love of the sport itself is the object, and competitive play is part of the game rather than the tool of politics or commerce.

PREFACE

This book originated as a series of lectures delivered at New College, University of New South Wales, in September 1999. Three years earlier I had been contacted by the Master of the College, Dr Allan Beavis, and informed that the lecture committee was looking for an assessment of the interaction of religion and sport with some reference to the forthcoming Sydney Olympic Games. At that time, I was working on a larger book focused on the nineteenth- and twentieth-century struggles of religious folk coming to terms with modern sport. My first impulse was simply to extract several chapters from that manuscript and insert some references to Australian sport and the Sydney Olympic Games.

That approach, though, seemed much too pedantic for the New College occasion. Moreover, those chapters pertained largely to American and British topics; unless they were considerably revised, they promised to be woefully unconnected to the forthcoming Sydney Olympics. Thus began my quest for a theme that would be both attractive and sufficiently provocative for public lectures. 'If Christ Came to the Sydney Olympics' seemed to meet those requirements.

For this publication, the Sydney reference has been dropped

from the title in order to make the book less constricted in time and place. For purposes of specificity, I have retained several of the original examples from Australian history and modern life, but must nevertheless beg the indulgence of Australian readers who will still find far too many references to 'Yankee' and 'Limey' data.

I am indebted, first of all, to Richard Cashman, Director of UNSW's Centre for Olympic Studies, who recommended me for this task and supported me throughout. His generosity included an armload of pertinent references, then a careful reading of this text. I am also grateful to Allan Beavis for his wonderfully informative and helpful correspondence which paved the way for my visit to Sydney, and for his cordial attention to my every need once I arrived. He restores one's faith in that good old term, 'a Christian gentleman'. His able colleagues at New College, Ian Walker, John Squires, Matthew Clarke and senior tutor Michael Choi, also aided me in numerous ways, especially in the provision of stimulating conversations.

Each evening before the public lectures, I dined with a select group of New College students, and one evening enjoyed an all-college banquet. Now, on the northeastern coast of the United States far removed from Sydney, I proudly wear a blue and white New College rugby jersey presented to me on the final night of my official duties. Thank you, New College students, for the warmth of your reception. This book is for you.

UNSW Press editor, Nada Madjar, made the book happen. Thank you Nada for your patient but persistent efficiency that turned a chore into a pleasure.

William J. Baker
Bass Harbor, Maine

BRINGING CHRIST TO THE OLYMPICS — AN EXERCISE IN IMAGINATION

I f Christ came to the Olympics? Putting the question of sport aside for the moment, Christians have not traditionally thought about Jesus in these terms. Never did Augustine of Hippo, St Thomas Aquinas, Martin Luther, John Calvin, John Wesley, Friedrich Schleiermacher or John Henry Newman imagine that Christ would truly reappear on earth except in glory at the end of the age. Much less were they willing to conjecture what Christ would think, say and do in certain literal situations. The cosmic Christ, for them, was too removed from the specifics of the historical Jesus, too exalted as the second person of the Trinity, too poised to return to earth in splendor, to imagine Him appearing in mundane, contemporary guise.[1]

LOOKING FOR JESUS

The nineteenth-century quest for the historical Jesus changed all that. Capping several decades of German critical scholarship, at the turn of the twentieth century Albert Schweitzer sought a profile of Jesus through the research of Biblical critics. Schweitzer came away baffled, concluding that the New Testament canon was constructed of disparate sources so tempered by earlier times and contradictory circumstances that we could never be certain what Jesus actually did and said.

Schweitzer found refuge in a kind of mystic imagination that affirmed the reappearance of Jesus whom he could never really find in religious writings:

> He comes to us as One unknown, without a name, as of old, by the lake-side, He came to those men who knew him not. He speaks to us the same word: 'Follow thou me!' and sets us to the tasks which he has to fulfill for our time.

As if he was foreseeing his own life of service in an African medical station, Schweitzer concluded about Christ:

> He commands. And to those who obey Him, whether they be wise or simple, He will reveal Himself in the toils, the conflicts, the

sufferings which they shall pass through in His fellowship, and, as an ineffable mystery, they shall learn in their own experience Who He is.[2]

If this sounds like poetry, so be it. Religion thrives best as poetry, not prose. When we confuse the two, we create problems for ourselves. Too much literalism creates an impediment — 'stumblingblock' is the old King James word for it — that makes it difficult for people to believe in God.

An American poet, James Russell Lowell, first voiced the idea of bringing a re-incarnated Christ to earth. Stepping beyond his Boston Brahmin heritage, the liberal Lowell envisaged Christianity as a call to minister to the less fortunate masses who toiled for adequate shelter, clothing and food. Lowell's Christ would deal with flesh-and-blood issues:

Said Christ our Lord, 'I will go and see
How the men, My brothers, believe in Me'.
He passed not again through the gate of birth,
But made Himself known to the children of earth.[3]

As one might anticipate, Lowell's Jesus turned away from 'the kingly fare' offered by political and ecclesiastical potentates, and from their rationalisation of a social system that sheltered the rich and crushed the poor. 'We build but as our fathers built', they explained in classic conservative terms. Lowell's Jesus would have none of it. Instead, He attended to the 'bitter groans' and salty tears of the outcast, and suggested that His followers do the same.[4]

A NEW WAY TO READ THE GOOD NEWS

An English journalist, William Thomas Stead, took the cue. In 1893–94 he made a six-month visit to Chicago, a dynamic city of great wealth but with dreadfully corrupt politics and monstrous tenement slums. Chicagoans Marshall Fields, Philip Armours and George Pullman prided themselves on hard work, economic success and generous philanthropy only to ignore the destitution close at hand. Catholic and Protestant church goers were little *social gospel*

better. If Christ came to Chicago, Stead concluded, he would turn from the churches to a reformed City Hall for the sanitation, minimum wage laws and educational opportunities necessary for Christianising the social order.[5]

Published in 1894 as a book of more than 400 pages, *If Christ Came to Chicago* stood at the forefront of an impressive bundle of books, sermons and essays representing the Social Gospel impulse to bring the Christian ethic into the backwaters and boardrooms of human life. In the very same year of Stead's publication, a Boston minister, Edward Everett Hale, saw his *If Jesus Came to Boston* appear in print. Around the turn of the twentieth century, parsons and lay people alike frequently conjectured about the prospect of Jesus coming into their towns, their places of business, their churches and their homes.[6]

I suspect few readers have come across these books, pamphlets or sermons. Perhaps, though, more have come into contact with another Social Gospel tract of the times: Charles Monroe Sheldon's novel, *In His Steps: What Would Jesus Do?* This little gem originated as a series of stories concocted for the young people in Sheldon's Central Congregational Church in Topeka, Kansas. In the story, the pastor responds imaginatively to a young man who asks what Jesus would do when confronted with unemployment, poverty, sour race relations and other problems of modern life. By the story's end, the congregation decides to apply their Christian principles to real life.

Charles Sheldon and William T. Stead were of the same mind in the meaning they assigned to Christ. 'For what He would have you do', in Stead's words, 'is to follow in His steps and be a Christ to those among whom you live, in the family, in the workshop, in the city and in the state.'[7]

This was a fashionable remedy for a world in which traditional religion had lost its savour. Within a year, *In His Steps* sold 100,000 copies, mostly in the United States, Britain, and English-speaking Canada, Australia and New Zealand. By the 1920s some fifty different publishers included twenty or so foreign translations in the distribution of more than 23 million copies of the book. By 1925 Sheldon could rightfully be astonished at the response of people 'all over the world of almost every tongue and tribe' to *In His Steps*.[8]

Only Bruce Barton rivalled Sheldon in the American marketplace. A son of a Congregationalist minister, Barton himself considered the Christian ministry but instead became a journalist and advertising executive. Most of all, he was an apologist for 'abundant living'. In place of the earnest, socially compassionate Jesus of the turn-of-century Social Gospel, Barton identified *A Young Man's Jesus* (1914) as a virile 'young man glowing with physical strength and the joy of living' who shared 'our bounding pulses, our hot desires' for wholesome pleasures. 'If there were a world's championship series in town', insisted Barton, 'we might look for Him there.'[9]

In *The Man Nobody Knows* (1925), Barton elaborated on Jesus as a sociable, vibrant personality whose 'consuming sincerity' would have made Him a highly successful businessman attuned to the consumer-oriented American scene of the 1920s. Jesus' appeal, insisted Barton, lay in His awareness that good salesmanship was of service to others. Corporate America gobbled up that gospel. Hollywood quickly turned *The Man Nobody Knows* into a film, and Cecil B. De Mille hired Barton as a consultant on *King of Kings* (1926), one of the first film spectaculars based on a Biblical theme. As one contemporary observed, Bruce Barton 'soaked the idea of success in the sanctity of the New Testament'.[10]

Barton also effectively bankrupted the tactic of imaginatively bringing Christ back to earth that we might grasp His message and do His bidding. In addition to the earlier Social Gospel Jesus, there had been a socialist Jesus and a radical revolutionary Jesus. Each one had met moral needs of the moment. Bruce Barton's Jesus, on the other hand, represented a new kind of morality: an

American optimistic success formula built on modern techniques of communication and persuasion.[11]

In his business hat, Barton called it advertising; in his pious mode, he called it evangelism. Billy Graham crusades and innumerable less polished forms of televangelism continue to promote the gospel according to Bruce Barton in the modern world.

WINDOWS AND MIRRORS

During the past fifty years or so, the tactic of bringing Christ to earth has gone topsy-turvy. Italian novelist Carlo Levi blazed the way in 1947 with *Christ Stopped at Eboli*. According to Italian local lore, 'Christ stopped just short of here, at Eboli', which meant that He never made it to a little remote village in southern Italy where Levi was exiled for his anti-fascist activities during World War 2. The absence of Christ metaphorically constituted an absence of any consciousness of good and evil, a scene bereft of hope and redemption. Perhaps it is significant that this famous conjecture about Christ coming to earth is, in fact, a metaphor for people living without Christ. He stopped at Eboli; He did not get to where we live.[12]

Nor did Christ make it to Limerick, Ireland, according to the sprightly logic of novelist Frank McCourt. In his memoir, *Angela's Ashes*, McCourt recalls a memorable moment from his childhood when one of his priestly teachers assigned an essay about 'what it would be like if our Lord had grown up in Limerick'. The teacher assumed that if Christ had lived in Limerick He would never have been crucified because the people of Limerick were such good Catholics. The young McCourt concurred, but only in part. If Christ had been born in Limerick, Frank McCourt admitted, He would never have grown up to die on the cross. In Limerick, He would have died in his cradle, of consumption, just like two of McCourt's brothers had died. Thus the youth of the world would be spared the bothersome imposition of confirmations, catechisms and communions.[13]

If this little thumbnail history of bringing Christ to earth is any guide to our present situation, the tactic of imagining Christ at the Olympics is fraught with problems. We run the risk of simply reading into the picture our own concerns and predispositions. We cannot escape this dilemma. Since the dawn of civilisation, we human beings have persistently created God in our own image. As Schweitzer warned us almost a century ago, each generation finds its own reflection in Jesus; each of us creates Christ in accordance with our own character.[14]

We especially tend to make Christ into a moralist who frowns upon the attitudes and behaviours we dislike, and applauds the values we affirm. Yet Christ is surely something more than a moralsmeister. If He came to the Olympics, His judgments about the 'good' and 'bad' aspects of the event might not be the most prominent — nor even the most significant — parts of His reactions to the Olympic scene. Keen-eyed, He would observe examples of historical change and sociological nuances. Sharp-minded, He would see connections on the one hand, disconnections on the other, between Olympic rhetoric and reality.

Christ need not fall prey to our post-modernist tendencies to gauge reality solely in self-referenced terms. Suffice it to say that we must admit the difficulties of sorting out what He would see, think, do and say, and must allow, as best we can, the Christ of our understanding to steer our path through the shoals of our own unspoken assumptions and passions. As novelist Reynolds Price puts it, our best hope of religious understanding and empathy lies in a 'restrained imagination' that 'thinks its way into the lives of others'.[15]

That is our ideal. Still, I hasten to remind, or warn, the reader that my Christ and I agree on most things. For reasons other than trinitarian orthodoxy, this enterprise requires a three-way interaction. In all the forthcoming theoretical and ethical issues surrounding the modern Olympics, I propose a tripartite conversation between author, reader and the Jesus whom we have come to know through the Gospels.

GODS AND GAMES — RELIGIOUS ASPECTS OF THE MODERN OLYMPICS

Nazareth was a 'hick town', an insignificant village far removed from the thoroughfare of ancient civilisation. Jesus of Nazareth, as Jaroslav Pelikan reminds us in his *Jesus Through the Centuries*, was 'a villager and a provincial', who seldom stepped beyond the confines of his home town. He seems never to have learned Greek or Latin, the two world languages of His day. For the metaphors that laced His conversations and preachments, He turned instinctively to sheep, shepherds, fields, trees and birds, not to larger regional or global issues.[1]

Unless the historical Jesus has been entirely replaced by a cosmic Christ unbound by time and mundane circumstance, the modern Olympics might well overwhelm Him. Cosmopolitan contexts of the past several Olympics — the media, complex transport systems, fine restaurants and bustling night life — have little in common with the small, quiet corner of the earth where Christ first appeared. He would most likely be awed by the huge crowds, technological innovations and organisational sophistication that characterise the modern Olympics.

Still, Christ would recognise ceremonies that are vaguely reminiscent of His own experience, not to mention the preoccupation of His followers through the ages. Olympic hymns, processions, liturgies, mythologies and proclamations resonate with traditional religious assertions of faith and hope.

MODERN GAMES

The modern Olympic Games are decidedly modern. At the most obvious level, they feature bicycle races, tennis matches, water events, team games and numerous other competitions that were totally absent from the ancient Olympics. Fibreglass equipment, synthetic uniforms and electronic timing devices all reflect the most up-to-date technologies. Bodies chiselled by scientific training techniques, regulated diets and (in some cases) performance-enhancing drugs push athletic capabilities to new heights. True to the name, Olympian athletes represent all the best and all the worst of modern athleticism.

Even more alien to a first-century Palestinian would be the complex communication and transportation systems which make the modern Games possible. The efficiency of faxes, emails and phones overwhelm even the hand-written letters and cablegrams employed by the late-Victorian founders of modern Olympism. From around the globe, athletes and spectators arrive by jet aircraft that dramatically supercede the old passenger ships on which Australia's gold medal winners Edwin Flack travelled to Athens in 1896 and Sydney native Freddie Lane to Paris in 1900.

Thanks to a television industry that has invaded the heavens for technological assistance, Olympic events are viewed around the world. They are beamed 'live' if we are lucky, and if we are patient enough to put up with commentators' verbiage that fills the gaps between events. At the least, the Games are taped and edited, ages removed from the earliest modern Games when not even action photography was readily available. In summary, the modern Games are more thoroughly organised, more effectively publicised and more commercialised than even Bruce Barton's entrepreneurial Jesus of the 1920s could have imagined.

The surest sign of modernity is a preoccupation with numbers. Organising committees eagerly count dollars and cents. What have we spent? What have we taken in? Amidst all the inevitable talk about the intangible spin-off benefits of the Olympics for the host city and nation, the bottom line is a number, not a value judgment. All the while, the number of athletes competing and the number of spectators in attendance are endlessly reported in the media.

Most of all, the numbers game is daily evident at the stadium as athletic records are set and broken. Sports scholars agree that the one feature of modern sport that distinguishes it from traditional or pre-modern athleticism is its mania for statistics and record-breaking performances. Whatever graceful athleticism is displayed in each event, the final word on the stadium scoreboard, in the press and in the television booth will pertain to a record broken or unbroken.[2]

All this records mania might be somewhat baffling for a Jesus whose numbers repertoire consisted merely of a few loaves and fishes.³ His disciples, not Jesus himself, estimated that a record-breaking crowd of 5000 enjoyed the fruit of their Master's blessing. At any rate, that 'multitude' of old would scarcely fill a tiny corner of any Olympic stadium. Beyond the matter of size, the sheer modernity of the Olympics separates them from the experience of the historical Jesus.

A MYSTIC BLEND

Yet for all its modernity, the Olympics would be recognisable to a person familiar with religious mythologies and ritual. Consider, especially, the highly orchestrated opening and closing ceremonies. Colourful processions, hymns, proclamations and oaths are reminiscent of a service of religious worship. To a remarkable extent, the modern Olympic Movement sustains a mystic blend of tones and textures originally found in old Hebrew temples, Catholic cathedrals and Protestant meeting houses.

The echoes are appropriate, for in the beginning religion gave birth to competitive athletics. Long before the birth of Christ, athletic contests originated as measures to please the gods. Victorious footraces, boxing bouts and chariot races supposedly insured good crops, healthy births and general good health. Archeologists are still uncovering ancient athletic arenas and ball courts adjacent to the priests' quarters.⁴

The religious origins of the ancient Greek Olympics are particularly well documented. Begun in 776 BC at the site of an old fertility cult devoted to the goddess Hera, the Greek Games honoured a newer and stronger male god, Zeus. In the name of Zeus, athletes took their oaths and won their crowns. Of the five-day festival that occurred every fourth year, half the time was devoted to religious sacrifice, hymns, processions and prayers.

When Christ ousted Zeus and other Graeco-Roman gods in the fourth century AD, the Greek Games were doomed to

extinction. By 500 or so, Olympia lay in ruins, soon to be sub-
merged by an earthquake and floods. But a strange thing happened on the way to the present circus. The road to the
twenty-first century is strewn with religious, especially Christian,
patronage of sport. Even medieval monks did it. As best we can
tell, they concocted an indoor handball game that evolved into
what we now know as tennis.[5]

Only the seventeenth-century Puritans mounted any serious
opposition to this marriage of sport and religion. To be sure, neither in England nor in North America did the Puritans act like
indiscriminate spoilsports. Their prohibitions were based on specific principles and fears. They abhorred old Catholic Church holidays,
when much sport was pursued in the early modern era. They held
Sunday sacrosanct, not to be desecrated by frivolous games. Most of
all, they detested gambling, which frequently accompanied sport.[6]

In the second half of the nineteenth century, religious folk
rediscovered sport, and with a vengeance. Liberal 'broad church'
Anglicans led the way. Charles Kingsley, a clergyman, novelist and
social reformer, headed a bevy of liberal church goers who not
only sought to become informed on the current intellectual, scientific and social issues of the day, but also preached the gospel of
physical and moral health to be found on fields of play. In 1874
Kingsley wrote that in cricket, football and the like, boys acquired
virtues which books could not give them. Sport inculcated in them

> not merely daring and endurance, but, better still, temper, self-
> restraint, fairness, honour, unenvious approbation of another's suc-
> cess and all that 'give and take' of life which stand a man in such good
> stead when he goes forth into the world, and without which, indeed,
> his success is always maimed and partial.[7]

In Britain's elite 'public' (private) schools, Anglican headmas-
ters soberly sought to inculcate 'godliness and good learning'. In
addition to the study of the classics, they emphasised rowing,
cricket and football as means of imparting principles of fair play

and, better still, team play. The purpose was moral: to make Christian gentlemen. Godliness, good learning and good games comprised a potent trinity in Victorian public schools.[8]

That package of religion and sport weighed heavily on all the political and economic factors that went into the making of the modern Olympics. In 1875 a twelve-year-old French youth read a translation of *Tom Brown's School Days*, a romanticised account of student life at Rugby School in England. The author, Thomas Hughes, attended Rugby School during the headmastership of the famous liberal Anglican, Dr Thomas Arnold. In truth, Arnold's tenure at Rugby (1828–42) predated the athletic binge that English public schools underwent in the mid-nineteenth century.[9]

When Hughes wrote *Tom Brown's School Days* in 1857, however, he idealised the stern, dutiful Arnold, unrealistically depicting him as a sports enthusiast. Misleading as it was, that image made a profound impression on its young French reader, Pierre de Coubertin, the future founder of the modern Olympic Movement.

In his early twenties, Coubertin made a pilgrimage to Rugby, and in the school chapel rhapsodised about the supposed vision of the virtuous Dr Arnold. Alone in the twilight, his eyes fixed on the funeral slab that bore the name of the great Arnold, Coubertin dreamed that he saw before him 'the cornerstone of the British Empire' that had been created by the comely mixture of piety and athletic prowess as espoused at Rugby and the other leading English public schools. 'If not quite a saint, Arnold became for Coubertin a kind of spiritual father figure,' comments historian Allen Guttmann.[10]

RELIGIOUS ATHLETICISM

Yet the religious flavour of Olympism as created by Coubertin required more than a dose of second-hand liberal Anglicanism. Equally important, and perhaps more so, was a French Catholic heritage that inspired Coubertin to think of sport as a kind of new religion with its own dogmas and rituals, 'but especially with religious feelings'.[11] His father, who came from a wealthy,

Catholic, royalist family, painted religious and patriotic themes; and his mother, the daughter of a marquis, was notably pious.

Encouraged by both parents to train for the Roman Catholic priesthood, Coubertin spent his early years at daily mass, catechisms and vespers in a French Jesuit school devoted to religious study. The scheme was derailed when he reacted against the Jesuits' repressive pedagogy and conservative curriculum that emphasised religion and the classics at the expense of modern, natural and social sciences. The would-be priest soon became skeptical of orthodox creeds. Tempted to atheism, he found refuge in the 'religion of humanity', a fashionable humanist philosophy espoused by a fellow Frenchman, Auguste Comte.[12]

Humanism, for Coubertin, did not exclude religious and moral concerns; rather, it intensified them and gave them new meanings in contemporary life. It also put him in awe of ancient Greek life and thought. Occasionally he even expressed admiration for old pre-classical fertility rites. In a piecemeal unscholarly fashion, Coubertin's thought reflected the new anthropological studies of his day. He was conversant with French and German versions of the great English anthropologist, James George Frazer, whose *Totemism* (1887) and multi-volume classic, *The Golden Bough* (1890, rewritten in 1911–15), attempted to make sense of ancient religious beliefs and systems of worship that revolved around seasonal rituals dramatising life and death issues.

When he explained why the modern Olympic Games should be held every fourth year, Coubertin could have simply cited the example of the ancient Greek Olympics. Instead, he wrapped his rationale in terms familiar to the anthropologists of his day. The modern Games should be celebrated every fourth year, Coubertin insisted, 'in a rhythm of astronomic rigidity, because they constitute the quarterly celebration of human springtime in honour of the constant renewal of mankind'.[13]

There is little wonder that one modern scholar considers Coubertin's 'peculiar religiosity' an exercise in elasticity that 'should not be mistaken for Christianity'. Little wonder, too, that Pope Pius X was at first suspicious of the 'pagan-seeming' character of modern Olympism. Not until 1906 — when French, Belgian and Italian athletes provided a private gymnastics exhibition at the Vatican — did the Pope give his blessing to Coubertin's creation.[14]

Lesser mortals did it earlier. Religious applause for the rebirth of the Olympics aptly began at the opening of the first modern Games, at Athens on 5 April 1896. That day was Easter Sunday for both Greek Orthodox and Roman Catholic branches of Christendom. The morning began with a holy mass for the athletes in the metropolitan cathedral, with the sermon preached by a French Dominican friar, Father Didon. At 11 am the Greek royal family and foreign princes arrived for a choir presentation of 'Te Deum'. At the stadium, opening ceremonies featured a newly-composed Olympic hymn to the 'Immortal Spirit of antiquity, father of the true, the good and the beautiful'.[15]

Both Catholic and Protestant prelates soon lined up to offer public prayers and sermons in celebration of the Olympics. In the opening ceremonies of the Stockholm Games of 1912, Sweden's royal pastor delivered a sermon in Swedish and a visiting Anglican said a prayer in English. The spectators then joined in the singing of Martin Luther's great hymn, 'Ein feste Burg ist unser Gott' ('A Mighty Fortress is Our God').[16] Eight years later, at Antwerp, the religious ceremony returned indoors for a 10 am service in Notre Dame Cathedral. As athletes filled the nave, Olympic officials and political authorities sat in the choir listening to a sermon by Cardinal Mercier, the Prelate of Belgium. Carefully avoiding controversy, Mercier urged his audience to exercise a sense of moderation and moral discipline in their athletic endeavours.[17]

Institutional religion would not be religion without sermons, it seems. Nor would Olympism. Of the innumerable sacred myths and sermonettes within the Olympic canon, none is more frequently intoned than an idealistic admonition to good sportsmanship. 'The important thing in the Olympic Games is not winning but taking part', Coubertin often preached in various combinations of phrases. 'The essential thing is not conquering but fighting well.'

Even this little homily has religious roots. Coubertin apparently took it directly from a sermon delivered by an American Episcopal bishop, the Right Reverend Ethelbert Talbot. In 1908 Talbot served as guest preacher at St Paul's Cathedral on the Sunday following the first week of the London Olympics. With athletes and Olympic officials present as guests of honour, Talbot lauded 'the great Olympic Games' for bringing robust youths together from all parts of the world. Nationalistic interests had caused several nasty disputes during the first week of competition, provoking Talbot to extol 'the exhilarating — I might also say soul-saving — interest that comes in active and fair and clean athletic sports'.

The remedy, insisted Bishop Talbot, lay in the amateur principle that the game itself is more valuable than the prize to be won: 'though only one may wear the laurel wreath, all may share the equal joy of the contest'. At those words Coubertin bolted upright in his pew. Over the next several years he publicly lauded Bishop Talbot's views as 'the foundation of a clear and sound philosophy' of Olympism: 'The importance of these Olympiads is not so much to win as to take part.'[18]

Amidst the bromides, Coubertin's secular, reconstructed faith inspired him to invest massive amounts of time, energy and money to create the modern Olympics. Like an evangelist, he preached his new gospel of sport. 'Have faith in it', he wrote to a friend, 'pour out your strength for it; make its hope your own.'[19]

Although a doctrinal renegade, Coubertin could not kick the habit of viewing the world in traditional religious terms. He saw athletes as 'new adepts', disciples of the new 'muscular religion'. He thought of spectators and coaches as 'the laity of sport'; quixotically he viewed the International Olympic Committee as 'a college of disinterested priests'. Olympic athletes, he insisted, should be 'imbued with a sense of the moral grandeur of the Games'; their 'vulgar competition' could be 'transformed, and in a sense sanctified' by contact with lofty sentiments.

In his very last public statement, a recorded message broadcast at the opening ceremony of the Berlin Games in 1936, Coubertin reiterated the 'religious sense' that lay at the heart of Olympism past and present. Though changed by time and circumstance, a religious spirit remained 'in essence the same as that which led the young Greeks, zealous for victory through the strength of their muscles, to the foot of the altar of Zeus'.[20]

Blessed by official Christendom, the quasi-religious aspects of the Olympic Movement exercised a mystic attraction for some individuals who had given up conventional religion. One true believer, Carl Diem, the German organiser of the 1936 Games, happily thought the solemnity and exuberance of the Berlin event 'equal to a church festivity'. The powerful president of the International Olympic Committee, Avery Brundage, depicted modern Olympism as 'a twentieth century religion, a religion with universal appeal which incorporates all the basic values of other religions, a modern, exciting, virile, dynamic religion, attractive to the youth'.[21]

Not a religious man in any orthodox sense of the term, Avery Brundage once mentioned his 'conversion, along with many others, to Coubertin's religion'. He certainly followed in the footsteps of the little French Baron in propounding a creed of fair play, good sportsmanship and amateur athletics. Brundage voiced his beliefs, as biographer Allen Guttmann tellingly puts it, as frequently and as earnestly 'as other clerics speak of the Immaculate Conception and the Virgin Birth'.[22]

SPLENDID CEREMONIES

More important than the beliefs — Olympic dogma or mythology, call it what you will — are the rituals that the modern Olympic Movement has created to impress itself upon a twentieth-century world. Again, Coubertin is the source. In constructing the trappings of Olympic festivals, he turned to the rites and ceremonies of his Catholic tradition: purposeful processions, oaths, hymns, invocations, myths, sacred sites, statues, wreaths and crowns. He imagined Olympic spectators like worshippers of old, exposed to a plethora of colourful sights and sounds that would, by repetition, achieve the status of ritual.[23]

There was method in this mania for ritual. 'If the modern Games are to exercise the influence I desire for them', Coubertin once wrote for the *Fortnightly Review*, 'they must in their turn show beauty and inspire reverence — a beauty and a reverence infinitely surpassing anything hitherto realised in the most important athletic contests of our day.' Beauty meant colourful buntings and flags, classical orchestras and popular band music, and choirs singing hymns of hope and joy. Evocative sights and sounds inspired reverence for the event: for the athleticism on display, and for the human spirit in its quest for excellence. In brief, concluded the little French Baron, 'the grandeur and dignity of processions' and 'the impressive splendor of ceremonies' made all the difference.[24]

If Christ came to the Olympics, He would be impressed with the grandeur and the splendour of the event, especially the semi- or quasi-religious atmosphere engendered. If we listen closely, however, we might hear Him remark that there is a difference between grandeur on the one hand, and glitz on the other. He might further remind us that splendour does not necessarily rhyme with spender, and that gaudiness is not godliness.[25]

Yet His response could well be like that of a young woman who worked for the International Olympic Committee in Switzerland. Interviewed by anthropologist John MacAloon, she admitted matter of factly that she 'didn't feel terribly excited or anything' when she first attended an Olympics event:

> I was sitting in the Opening Ceremony and I couldn't believe it. When the torch bearer came into the stadium and the crowd roared, I suddenly began to cry. I remember thinking, 'So this is what it's all about!' I don't think I'll ever forget that moment as long as I live.[26]

For Christ, too, the opening and closing ceremonies might well be events most memorable.

For the first modern Olympics, at Athens in 1896,
Pierre de Coubertin, founder of the modern
Olympic Movement, insisted on the abundant
display of national flags to rekindle the flame of
devotion and adequately honour a victorious
athlete. The same ritual has been repeated
till present day, as seen here at the opening
ceremony of the 1984 Olympics where the
audience held up cards to depict flags of all
participating countries.
(courtesy of Amateur Athletic Foundation)

GOOD GAMES — AFFIRMING THE ATHLETIC PLEASURES OF THE FLESH

I magine Christ at an Olympic stadium on the first day of athletic competition. As He takes His seat in the warmth of the morning sun, He recalls the quasi-religious spectacle of the day before: the orderly march of athletes into the stadium, all aglow with youthful pride and expectant spirit; the procession of national flags and anthems, emblems and costumes; the Olympic flag with its five colourful interlocking rings on a white background, towering above all the national flags to the accompaniment of the Olympic hymn; the arrival of the sacred flame, lit at Olympia and carried to the host city with extravagant fanfare, to remain here for a fortnight; the head of the host nation pronouncing the official formula that opens the Games.

Then, Christ now recalls a day later, the mood shifted from one of high solemnity to an atmosphere of sheer joy and excitement. A splendid program of choreographed music and dance closed out the day.

That was yesterday. Today, Christ senses yet another mood in the stadium. Festival has given way to competitive intensity. Yesterday the athletes came decked out in fashionable suits and ties, sashes and ribbons, spit and polish; today they are stripped for action. The Games with a capital G began yesterday, or last year when they were being orchestrated; the games *per se*, the athletic contests, now begin.

STRIPPED FOR ACTION

As the athletes take the field seriously focused on the business at hand, their near-nakedness is the first thing that impresses Christ. Some wear shorts and tank shirts; others wear colourful skintight body suits. Short and tall, thin and hefty, none can hide from public view in these skimpy costumes.

Christ is reminded of the athletic attire, or total lack of it, in the Greek Olympics of His own day. He only heard rumours about them, of course. To the best of our knowledge, He never made the arduous sea voyage across the eastern Mediterranean to Olympia. Had He done so, He would have stood amidst some

30,000 or 40,000 people on the embankment surrounding the grounds where athletic contests took place in the scorching heat of a Greek mid-summer day. He would have witnessed a remarkable sight of stark nude athletes, all of them male, running, jumping, throwing the discus and javelin. As wrestlers groped and boxers feinted for advantage, the admonition not to hit below the belt was lost on first-century Olympic competitors.

Surely Christ heard about some Jewish boys of His day who shocked their elders by staging Greek-style athletic contests of their own. Worst of all, or best of all for its shock value in a conservative world of Sadducees and Pharisees, they even mimed the Greeks by competing in the nude. A few Graeco maniacs went so far as to seek cosmetic surgery to conceal their circumcision, a telltale tribal sign of their 'barbarian' non-Greek origins.

Not completely nude, the lightly clad athletes at the modern Olympics are bodies in motion. No less purposeful than Olympians of old, they run, jump, lift, tumble, balance, grapple, flail, glide and plunge. They glisten with sweat as they push themselves (in the words of the Olympic motto) to faster, higher and stronger feats of physical achievement. In prolonged vigorous events such as the distance footraces, by the end of the ordeal they are bent over, gasping for air. According to how well they do, they grimace or laugh or weep. Between events, some turn to colleagues for encouragement; others turn inward to tap fresh sources of strength.

But are these not the 'druggies' that the media make so much of? Is the world of Olympian athletic achievement really a scene from the 1950s movie, *The Invasion of the Body Snatchers*, where reasonably attractive, normal-looking bodies have been taken over by an alien power invisible to the naked eye? In the case of these athletes, the alien is an artificial hormone, anabolic steroids.

At the Seoul Olympics in 1988, one of those wonderfully chiselled bodies turned out to be chock-full of steroids. Having won the 100 meters in 9.79 seconds, Canada's Ben Johnson tested

positive for drug use and was disqualified amidst a global out-
burst of dismay. Investigators implicated Johnson's coach,
Charles Francis, who confessed that no fewer than thirteen of his
Canadian athletes, male and female, were on prohibited drugs.
Yet Canada, one suspects, was no worse, if no better, than most
other nations eager to ring the Olympic bells.

At Christ's first exposure to the Games, though, I propose
that we praise the Olympics, not bury them. Leave the negative
aspects for future discourse. For now, I prefer to run the risk of
appearing Pollyanna-like by singing the praise of the positive.

Of the several positives that come immediately to mind, none
are the ones most often paraded by official Olympic rhetoric. For
example, international understanding and goodwill were para-
mount motivators in Coubertin's original scheme, and remain
dominant in the lexicon of Olympism. In truth, though, the
modern Olympics have served as occasions for as much discord as
concord. Arguably, they have intensified and prolonged more
international disputes than they have resolved.[1]

I do not wish to join that 'army of nincompoops' identified
by John Lucas as people who 'have served up a non-directed,
inflammatory mishmash of "incidents" that have taken place' at
the Olympics.[2] Lucas is referring to incidents that reflect poorly
on the Olympics, of course. Such protestations notwithstanding,
nasty Anglo-American squabbles at London in 1908, the bloody
water polo game at Melbourne in 1956, and the hostage tragedy
at Munich in 1972 stand as merely three of many ugly incidents
that give the lie to the rhetoric of international understanding
and goodwill. Global pacification is not the hook on which we
need to hang our praise.

But there are others, I suggest three, all pertaining to the athletes themselves. More precisely, they all pertain to a gradual
broadening of the definition of athletic eligibility. The question
of who can play bears directly upon the question of how they
play, and even how well they play. Christ at Athens in 2004 might

well be relieved that He is here, and not at the Athens Games in 1896, because the athletic performances here are incomparably better and most definitely more interesting.

AMATEUR NO MORE

The Olympics now feature the best athletes in the world regardless of their social status. It was not always this way. The original amateur code favoured the well-born and well-bred: those whose papas and mamas provided expense accounts that paid for any training, travel or medical needs, not to mention the daily stuff of food and shelter. To demand pay for play was to display one's inferior social origins. Thus the great preponderance of those who went for gold in the early Olympics had silver spoons in their mouths. One runner literally wore white gloves.

Silver spoons and white gloves make good amateurs but not necessarily good athletes. The wearer of the white gloves, a Frenchman, ran both the 100 metres and the marathon at Athens in 1896. When asked by an English-speaking journalist how he trained for such dissimilar races, he reportedly explained, 'One day, I run a leetle way, vairy queek. Ze next day, I run a long way, vairy slow.'[3] That's amateurism for you.

The early Games were so exclusively confined to middle- and upper-class competitors that the occasional commoner who slipped under the wire called attention to himself, especially if he won. When a Greek shepherd, Spiridon Loues, won the marathon at Athens, crown princes ran jubilantly beside him to the finish line. Loues instantly became a national hero, and reaped appropriate benefits. Proud, grateful Greeks gave him gold watches and chains, suits of clothes, free restaurant meals, and more drachmas than he could imagine spending in a whole lifetime. Alarmed at all this deluge of material profit, Olympic officials spread the word that Loues refused the gifts. As Coubertin moralised, Loues' refusal to capitalise on his athletic feat 'saved the non-professional spirit from a very great danger'.[4]

In 1912 the guardians of that 'non-professional spirit' dealt harshly with yet another alien who slipped into their classy club-room. The offender was none other than a stocky, heavy-jowled, rough-mannered American Indian, Jim Thorpe, who won the gold in both the decathlon and pentathlon at Stockholm. The King of Sweden personally congratulated Thorpe as 'the greatest athlete in the world'. Thorpe reportedly replied with a spontaneity that would have made an informal Australian happy: 'Thanks, King'. Yet six months later Thorpe was stripped of his Olympic medals when it became known that he had received money for playing minor league baseball prior to his Stockholm achievements.

One more dismal example of the reign of King Amateur will suffice. In 1932 the most famous runner in the world, Finland's Paavo Nurmi, was disqualified on the eve of the Los Angeles Olympics for having accepted monetary compensation for his track skills. In the three previous Olympics, Nurmi had won seven golds and three silvers in the ten long-distances races he entered; he held dozens of world records. But none of that mattered. 'Nurmi', said one Olympic official, 'had the lowest heart beat and the highest asking price of any athlete in the world.'[5] That was enough to get him expelled from the gentlemen's amateur club.

It was a quirky club with some quirky rules that often made no pretence of being based on anything other than social prejudice. For equestrian sports, for example, it arbitrarily defined military officers as amateurs and ordinary soldiers as professionals. For the London Games of 1948, a Swedish cavalryman who happened to be an expert horseman was promoted from sergeant to lieutenant by royal decree to make him eligible to represent Sweden. Once the Games were finished, he was demoted to his previous rank. Bad publicity caused a revision in the rules prior to the Helsinki Games of 1952, when that same Swedish sergeant, unpromoted, won a gold medal.[6]

For Baron Pierre de Coubertin and his hand-picked cadre of socially elite members of the International Olympic Committee (IOC) in its early years, the amateur dogma made solid sense. It rang true to their upper-class origins and assumptions. Avery Brundage, President of the IOC from 1952 to 1972, was more dogmatic, however. A self-made American millionaire, Brundage was a passionate and unyielding defender of the amateur code. 'He preached amateurism like an apostle of a religion', said Geoffrey Miller, 'and skirmished like a knight of King Arthur defending the Holy Grail.'[7]

Preach and skirmish as he might, Brundage's amateur ideals got crushed between two opposite (and opposing) forces. The first was American university athletic scholarships that essentially paid for room, board and tuition, allowing college athletes to train and perform regardless of their family's ability to pay. As early as 1928 the British press complained about this peculiar form of subsidy as a dire threat to amateurism.[8]

A more ominous threat came from the Soviet Union, where athletic endeavours fed off a complex system of state support through military, police and educational units. After the Soviets and their communist bloc friends swept the boards at Melbourne in 1956, the days of Olympic amateurism were numbered.

Brundage fought it to the end. Just before he retired from the IOC presidency in 1972, he castigated alpine skiers for the commercial deals they had cut with equipment companies. Not half the French team was living up to the amateur rule, Brundage complained. 'You have been misinformed, Monsieur', replied a member of the French Olympic Committee. 'No one on the French team lives up to your definition.'[9]

Not for long would anyone try. When Ireland's Lord Killanin succeeded Brundage in 1972, he saw the amateur question as an item long overdue on the Olympic agenda. Haltingly he announced:

I do not believe in professional Olympics; I do not believe in open Olympics; but I think we have to realise that we are about to enter the last quarter of the twentieth century.[10]

That meant many things, but especially a kind of democratisation of Olympic opportunity. By 1978 track-and-field athletes could earn money for their clubs so long as they did not take direct personal payments. By 1982 the rules were again changed to allow payment into a trust fund from which athletes could draw expense money during their athletic careers, and substantial payoffs thereafter. By the 1988 Games, the Olympics were open to virtually everyone except professional boxers, NBA basketball players and soccer players over the age of twenty-three. Four years later, even NBA players became eligible. Allen Guttmann summarised the early 1990s scene thus:

Olympic athletes were free, at last, of the hypocritical need to pretend that they were really just ordinary blokes who trained a bit after work.[11]

What are we to make of these changes? Do they represent wholesome progress, or should we see them as erosion of an important athletic principle? How would Christ view them if He came to Sydney? Let me remind you that you have been forewarned: My Christ and I tend to agree on most matters.

This one thing I know: Christ hated hypocrisy, in whatever guise He found it. The amateur code was hypocritical from the outset, claiming to be something it was not. It claimed to be about keeping athletic competition pure by prohibiting payment for pay; in truth, it was an ingenious method of protecting an upper-class citadel against the invasion of the 'barbarian hordes'.

Moreover, guardians of the amateur code claimed to have a clear definition of their treasure, but in fact they increasingly held onto a figment of their own imagination, blurred beyond recognition. I can scarcely believe that any Christ of truth and clarity would lament the passing of such a hazy distortion of truth.

Whether Christ agrees with me or not, I applaud the Olympics for opening up the Games to the best athletes from around the world.

ENTER THE WOMEN

Another good game worthy of applause is the gender game that the Olympics have played out over the past fifty years or so. Ancient Olympic officials, of course, sternly forbade women competitors. Despite the fact that pre-Olympian games were promoted at Olympia in honour of the goddess Hera, even female spectators were banned from the precincts once the men took over. More to the point, the fathers of modern Olympism (Coubertin especially) shared the prejudices of their age concerning female athletes. Not a single women's event was on the program at Athens in 1896.[12]

The first seven Olympiads saw a mere trickle of female golfers, tennis players, archers, figure skaters, swimmers and divers. In 1912 two Australian women, Sarah 'Fanny' Durack and Wilhelmina 'Mina' Wylie had to find their own funds to pay for travel to Stockholm and were able to go only after some prominent women raised a public subscription. That year Durack won gold and Wylie took the silver in the 100-metre swimming event, while Australia's entire 26-member men's team won exactly the same number of gold and silver medals — one of each.[13]

But track-and-field athletics were the core of the Olympic program, and male Olympic officials fiercely resisted allowing women to run, jump and throw competitively. Opposition also came from quite unexpected quarters. Female physical educators in the United States controlled college sport for women and shuddered at the prospect of women's sport going the commercialised way of men's intercollegiate athletics. For years they fought against American women participating in the Olympics.[14]

So did Rose Scott, a leading feminist and suffragist in New South Wales. Athletic competition, she feared, would banish the

Sarah 'Fanny' Durack (left) and Wilhelmina 'Mina'
Wylie (centre) won (respectively) gold and silver
medals in 100-metres freestyle at Stockholm
Olympics in 1912. They had to find their own funds
to go to the Olympics even though the entire men's
team of 26 won the same number of gold and silver
medals — one of each. (Ian Gordon)

decorum necessary for women to survive in a world dominated by men. She especially recoiled against the prospect of half-clad women swimmers competing in front of 'a lot of bad men' who would 'go rather for the spectacle than for the skill' and 'make all sorts of nasty remarks'. As is clear, male resistance is not the whole story of the slow entrance of women into Olympic competition.[15]

In 1921, though, some European women initiated an international federation of sportswomen, and within the next year produced a Women's Olympic Games in Paris. Under protest from the IOC, the word 'Olympic' was dropped, but from 1922 to 1934 four highly successful Women's World Games featured basketball and strenuous track events in addition to the usual ladies' fare. Faced with these counter-attractions, the IOC agreed to include women's track-and-field in the program at Amsterdam in 1928.[16]

Doubting Thomases had their doubts confirmed in a bizarre finish to Amsterdam's 800-meter race for women. A German woman won in world record time, but just over the finish line virtually every one of her competitors sprawled exhausted onto the cinder track, gasping for air. The press eagerly reported the spectacle of 'wretched women' and 'knocked out and hysterical females floundering all over the place', supposedly unable to endure such strenuous competition. This little episode spawned yet another argument over the legitimate role of women in Olympic sports. The 800 metres for women disappeared from the Olympic program, not to reappear until 1960.[17]

What credibility the Amsterdam fiasco damaged in 1928, Mildred 'Babe' Didrikson repaired at Los Angeles in 1932. Probably the best all-round female athlete of the twentieth century, she set world or Olympic records in the 80 metres, the javelin and the high jump. Without doubt, she was the brightest of all the stars, male or female, at Los Angeles in 1932. Better still, she was a working-class Texan, strong-willed and crude of manners, and a self-styled tomboy to boot.[18]

Mildred 'Babe' Didrikson, probably the best all-round female athlete of the twentieth century and the star at the 1932 Olympics in Los Angeles, where she set world or Olympic records in the 80 metres, the javelin and the high jump. (courtesy of Amateur Athletic Foundation)

Yet Babe Didrikson was an exception, not a rule, for female Olympic athletes prior to World War 2. The Cold War made all the difference, especially for women athletes in the West. At the very first Olympics in which the Soviets competed, at Helsinki in 1952, it quickly became evident that Soviet male athletes were roughly on a par with their Western counterparts, but that Soviet women were something else. Especially in gymnastics and track-and-field events, Soviet women simply overwhelmed their American, British and West German competitors.

Curiously, only Australian women held their own. At Helsinki, Australian runners Marjorie Jackson and Shirley Strickland set world records respectively in the 100-metre and 200-metre races, and in the 80-metre hurdles. Four years later 'the magic came to Melbourne'. In Australia's first outing as an Olympic host, Strickland repeated her 1952 victory in the 80-metre hurdles, seventeen-year-old 'golden girl' Betty Cuthbert won the 100-metre and 200-metre races, and swimmers Dawn Fraser, Lorraine Crapp, Faith Leech and Sandra Morgan dominated the pool events.[19]

Still, the Russians had come, and they stayed to conquer. From the Helsinki Games in 1952 through to the Moscow Olympics of 1980, Soviet and Soviet-bloc women increasingly collected most of the medals awarded. The Russian strategy, to be blunt, was to have their men strive for parity with the West, and to leave it to the women to insure victory in the point totals. At Montreal in 1976, this tactic produced gold medals for Eastern European women in forty-four of the forty-nine women's events. Rumours abounded regarding the use of steroids and other illegal drugs, especially by East German women swimmers. But the fact remained that their scientific exercise, diet and weight-training programs were demonstrably superior to the investments made in women of the West.[20]

For Americans, especially, this disparity brought the issue of women's sports to the fore. Arguably, the Cold War was more

'Golden girl' Betty Cuthbert in training. In 1956. Aged seventeen, she won gold in the 100-metres and 200-metres, races at the Melbourne Olympics. (Cuthbert and Webster, *The Golden Girl*).

Opposite Marjorie Jackson, the 'Lithgow Flash', set a new world record for 200 metres at the 1952 Olympics in Helsinki. (News Limited)

important than the feminist movement of the 1960s or Title IX legislation in 1972 (requiring equal opportunity for women's athletic programs at institutions supported by federal funds) in preparing American women for Olympic competition. Like nothing else, Cold War pressures focused American commitment on the recruitment and preparation of female athletes. Otherwise, Wilma Rudolph might never have achieved recognition as a world-class sprinter, as she did at Rome in 1960. Nor would Florence Griffith-Joyner have emerged as a fantastically fast, flambouyant sprinter at Seoul in 1988.

Suffice it to say that if Christ came to the Olympics, He would note numerous women participants among the athletic crowd. The Atlanta Games of 1996 saw some 3700 females (36 per cent of all the athletes) compete, about 1000 more than at Barcelona four years earlier. Surely an irony involving Christ's number one opponent, Muhammad, would be apparent: Islamic dress codes prevented twenty-seven nations from sending female athletes to the Atlanta Olympics.[21]

ADDING COLOUR

Himself barely Caucasian, Christ would be impressed with the athletes' many shades of colour. In His own day, only the Roman games featured non-European competitors. African and near-Eastern slaves or captives of war literally fought for their lives in the Colosseum. The ancient Greek Olympics, on the other hand, limited their competitive rosters to free-born Greeks. In banning foreign 'barbarians', they kept their games white except for Mediterranean sun-tans.

To the great credit of modern Olympic leaders, race has never been a prohibitive factor in the admission of athletes to the Games. In fact, Baron Pierre de Coubertin sought to prepare African athletes for Olympic competition by arranging All-African games at Algiers in 1925 and in Alexandria in 1929. Only the poverty of emerging nations or the racism of a few national

Florence Griffith-Joyner at
the 1988 Olympics in
Seoul after winning
women's 4 × 400-metres
relay race. (photograph by
Tony Duffy, Allsport)

Olympic committees has kept Olympic doors closed to people of colour.

Africa illustrates both of these problems. Beginning in 1912, several Egyptian and French colonial athletes regularly competed in the Olympics, but not until 1960 did a black African (marathoner Abebe Bikila of Ethiopia) win a gold medal. Of the eight marathon competitors at those Rome Olympics, four were Africans.[22] As independent African nations have achieved economic stability, they have increasingly sent teams to the Olympics. From 1968 to 1996 Kenyan runners won no fewer than eleven gold medals in the 1500-metre to 10,000-metre races. Of the fifty-two African states represented at the Atlanta Olympics in 1996, thirty-four won medals, including eleven golds.[23]

The politics of racial prejudice within various national Olympic committees have been even more prohibitive than economic factors. South Africa is a prime example, but first we would do well to consider American and Australian racial scorecards. The saga of Jesse Owens and the dominance of African-American Olympians since World War 2 blur the edges of a dismal picture of American racism prior to the 1930s. Jim Crow sat noisily and nastily on the shoulders of most American athletic events, especially team sports. Until the politically charged atmosphere leading to the 1936 Nazi Olympics, the total number of African-American Olympians was minuscule.

Australian Aborigines did not fare any better. Although Aborigines dominated 'pedestrianism' around the turn of the last century and frequently won early regional events such as the Stawell Gift and Burnie and Bendigo foot-races, we can count on a single hand the Aboriginal athletes who have represented Australia in the Olympics. Necessarily professional when professionalism was a bad word in the Anglo-Saxon lexicon, often they still lack access to the right clubs, to the necessary equipment and coaching that would put them on a par with other Australians, much less on the same Olympic team.[24]

Still, for much of the twentieth century South Africa stood out as the sorest thumb of all in black-white race relations. Although South African sport and Olympic teams were no better and no worse than the rigidly segregated society of which they were a part, their Apartheid was a sure-fire target of dispute after 1960, 'the year of Africa', when Bikila won gold in the marathon at Rome and no fewer than sixteen new African nations won independence from European rule. In 1963 Adetokunbo Ademola of Nigeria became the first black African member of IOC.[25]

Under pressure from new black African nations, the IOC excluded South Africa from the 1964 Tokyo Olympics, but then voted to lift the ban for the Mexico City Games four years later. Black Africa, supported by the Soviet Union, reacted furiously. The threat of a boycott by thirty-two African nations caused the IOC to reverse its decision, barring South Africa from the 1968 Mexico City Games. In 1970 South Africa was expelled from the Olympic Movement altogether, effectively isolating her for more than two decades.[26]

Arguably, sport played an important part in the larger national and international struggles that led to the early 1990s, when South Africa began dismantling its racial barriers.[27] Only twenty years earlier, we would not have predicted such a change, especially without massive bloodshed. The appearance of black South African athletes at Sydney in 2000 and at Athens in 2004 will constitute a modern marvel. If Christ attends, I am certain He will applaud it as a miraculous event more important than turning water into wine.

THE POWERS AND THE GLORY — GOING FOR GOLD AND OTHER FALSE GODS

Jesus of Nazareth blessed the poor, healed the sick and consoled the broken-hearted. He also lauded generosity of spirit and gestures of courage and kindness. Yet He was no Pollyanna. He expressed dismay at the prospect of limited vision crimping people's lives. He detested hypocrisy, and on several occasions warned of divine judgment against the unrighteous. Once He even angrily took the whip to some money changers who were defiling the temple with their greed.

If Christ came to the Olympics, He would be impressed with quasi-religious aspects of Olympic rituals and sterling athletic performances on the field, but He would also be uneasy with some less positive features of the Games. He might well be inspired to bring out His whip against the modern scene, for he would most certainly recognise some idolatrous tendencies embedded in today's Olympism.

Idolatry is the worship of a god, or gods, of one's own making. In traditional Judaeo-Christian terms, it is the bowing of the heart to any person, object or enterprise other than the Lord God Jehovah. As William T. Stead reminded us many years ago, religious hymns, prayers and sermons 'may or may not have a close and living connection with your religion', nor does worship 'necessarily imply genuflections, kowtowing and chin-chinning oriental fashion'. According to Stead,

> You worship what you consciously or unconsciously set before yourself as the ideal toward which you aim, the model according to which you endeavour to fashion your life.[1]

These words from *If Christ Came to Chicago* first appeared in print in 1894, just two years before the opening of the first modern Olympic Games.

PAYING THE PIPER

Amidst all the false gods that jockey for dominance at the Olympics, commercialism stands tall. In its mildest, most innocuous form, a cash-nexus mentality interacts with traditional

Olympic idealism, determining where and how the quadrennial Games are held, and the manner in which they are presented to the world through the press and television. Corruption lurks just beneath the surface of that arrangement as rules get bent and dirty dollars get spent at the commercial altar.

Scarcely can the roots of this problem be traced to Baron de Coubertin, at least not directly. His aristocratic background bred disdain for industrialisation and commerce. Coubertin instinctively detested 'the material powers' that seemed to rise 'like Cyclopean ramparts' around people in the late nineteenth century. Sport, he believed, could serve as a moral counterpoint, an idealistic antidote to the materialistic tendencies of modern life. Most of all, Coubertin wanted to endow sport with a moral basis that would prevent its being 'commercially exploited by the organisers of public exhibitions'.[2]

For practical reasons, however, three of the first four Olympics were appended to circus-like expositions devoted to the display of scientific, industrial and commercial progress. The 1900 Games were something of a sideshow to the Paris Universal Exhibition. Worse still, the 1904 Games saw athletes compete amidst freak shows, anthropological displays, and agricultural and industrial equipment at the St Louis World Fair. The London Games of 1908 were held in conjunction with an Anglo-French exhibition.[3]

These expositions guaranteed some credibility and press coverage; they also provided financial assistance and spectators who might not have otherwise turned out for the athletic events. Once it was disengaged from industrial exhibitions (beginning with the Stockholm Games of 1912), Olympism quickly grew to maturity holding to the twin anti-commercial principles of its founder — athletic competition confined to amateurs, and Games organised and promoted under the careful, conservative supervision of the International Olympic Committee (IOC).

Avery Brundage, who became a member of the IOC in 1936

and served as its president from 1952 to 1972, momentarily kept the commercial forces at bay. As biographer Allen Guttmann explains, Brundage adamantly resisted his 'religion of Olympism' being defiled by athletes taking money to advertise their equipment or garb before television cameras. 'Brundage looked upon the fallen athletes as sinners or, when they openly defied him and boasted of their commercialism, as apostates.' Worse still, he considered it 'blasphemy' to appropriate the Olympic motto and emblems for any purpose other than the enhancement of the Olympic Movement.[4]

All that has changed since Brundage's presidency. The dismantling of the amateur code is most certainly a factor in this change. For athletes now to go literally for the gold in the form of hard cash is to bring commercialism into full view. More importantly, an Olympic gold medal is a ticket to lucrative appearance fees, product endorsements and job assignments. As Canadian critics Richard Gruneau and Hart Cantelon shrewdly put it, today 'the race for sponsorship and endorsements, both by athletes and Olympic organisers', takes on 'greater importance than the eventual race for the finish line'.[5]

Corporate involvement is another crucial component in the story of Olympic commercialisation. Prior to the 1970s, the expenses of building athletic venues and quarters to house the athletes fell largely on national and local governments, supplemented by private philanthropy. In most cases, old stadiums were given face-lifts and Olympic villages were built as economically as possible. Government involvement in the form of subsidies and tax-breaks is still essential, of course, but one cannot imagine today's Olympics without heavy investment from corporate sponsors.

This quiet revolution did not occur overnight. As early as 1928, Coca Cola paid for the right to associate their product with the Olympics, and in the early 1960s began shelling out big money for the right to advertise Coke as the official Olympic soft drink. At the Melbourne Games in 1956, Horst Dassler began asking both athletes and Olympic officials to display his Adidas footwear for a financial return. By the 1970s, Adidas reigned as the corporate power behind the Olympic rings.[6]

The Los Angeles Games of 1984 represent something of a milestone in the history of commercialised sport. At the head of the Los Angeles Olympic Organising Committee stood a bold and able businessman, Peter Ueberroth. Impressed with the fact that since 1932 every Olympiad except one had lost money, Ueberroth was determined not merely to avoid a loss but rather to run the Games at a profit. To that end, he raised $130 million from thirty corporate sponsors, including Coca Cola, McDonald's, American Express, Anheiser-Busch, Canon, IBM, Levi's and Atlantic Richfield. In a sterling example of commercial excess making for personal success, Ueberroth gave himself a bonus of nearly half a million dollars from a surplus (profit) that exceeded $200 million.[7]

In addition to his line-up of corporate sponsors, Ueberroth negotiated a $225 million contract with ABC for American television rights. European and Asian networks chipped in another $33 million, establishing the media as the largest of all the corporate sponsors of Olympism.

They who pay the piper, call the tune. Given the massive corporate investment in recent Olympics, we should not be surprised at the highly commercialised atmosphere surrounding the Games. Today, commercialised Olympism ultimately depends on the golden horn of television. Television fees fill the Olympic coffers and at the same time provide a captivated audience for the advertising of sponsors' wares.

At the Winter Olympics in 1968, Avery Brundage complained bitterly as skiers and ice-skaters craftily displayed their sponsors' logos to the television cameras. For the stern Brundage, that hucksterism appeared to be nothing more than 'Olympic butter, Olympic sugar, Olympic petrol'.[8] Had he lived long enough to witness the commercial circuses of the 1980s and 1990s, his blood pressure would have shot through the roof.

Christ, too, might well be advised to take an aspirin before He attends an Olympics event. Otherwise, His spirit will be swamped with what William T. Stead called 'the idols of the market place'.

PATRIOTIC GAMES

The nation state is another idol frequently enthroned at the Olympics. As chauvinist pride propels athletes to victory, patriotic flags and national anthems dominate the awards ceremonies. All the while, jingoistic bias colours both press and television commentary.

From the outset, the modern Olympics were conceived in the womb of rabid nationalism. Baron de Coubertin was an impressionable seven year old when France suffered a crushing defeat at the hands of a Prussian army in the Franco-Prussian War of 1870. Seized with spasms of shame and resentment, Coubertin and his cohorts seethed with revenge. Moreover, as he entered adulthood, France aggressively competed against German and British imperial interests in Africa and the Far East. Preachments about racial pride, national vigour and physical prowess filled the political speeches and literature of that day.

Coubertin steered perilously close to viewing patriotism as the modern equivalent of religious piety. He framed the issue in his final recorded speech for the Berlin Games in 1936:

> The contestants of the ancient world formed their bodies in the gymnasium just as the sculptor formed statues in his workshop, and both in doing so did honour to the gods. The modern athlete likewise does honour to his country, to his race, to his flag.[9]

For the very first modern Games, in Athens in 1896, Coubertin insisted on the abundant display of national flags as

Cathy Freeman carrying
the Australian and the
Aboriginal flags in 1994.
(Craig Golding/Sydney
Morning Herald)

the one thing that could rekindle the flame of devotion and adequately honour a victorious athlete. This tendency to deify the
nation state and its symbols made Couberin a distinctly modern,
secularised man. At worst, he sounded like a fascist; at the least,
Coubertin was a fervent French patriot. Coubertin made a dis-
tinction, however, between patriotism and nationalism. He
extolled patriotism as the love of one's own country and the
unselfish desire to serve her; he rejected the nationalism that
hated other countries and sought to do them harm.[10]

In good nineteenth-century European liberal terms,
Coubertin loathed war, thinking it an irrational throwback to
primitive barbarism. Other liberals wanted to replace war with
negotiations and unfettered economic competition (free trade);
Coubertin thought international athletic competition was the
solution. In his optimistic vision, quadrennial Olympic gatherings
would foster international understanding, tolerance and peace.
Patriotism, he insisted, was a good thing so long as it was muted
in Olympism's 'peaceful and chivalrous contests' that would
transform nationalism into 'the best of internationalisms'.[11]

In its best moments, modern Olympism has fulfilled these
heady dreams. Although the swords have yet to be turned into
plowshares, the Olympic 'sacred truce' has brought together
French and German, American and Russian, and even Kenyan
and white South African athletes to compete fiercely but fairly.

Each Olympiad produces its own examples of the understanding and goodwill that periodically transcend ideological, racial and
linguistic barriers when athletes convene under the five-ringed
Olympic flag. The more intense the nationalistic conflict, the
more heart-warming the tales of friendship. My favourite comes
from the Berlin Games of 1936, when a blond German long-
jumper, Lutz Long, demonstratively befriended a black American
star, Jesse Owens, right under the racist nose of the Reichsführer.

Beyond the anecdotes, the Olympic saga is filled with scenes
of simple patriotic pride in one's own country. Smartly dressed

PRIME TIME PROSELYTES— EVANGELICALS AT THE OLYMPICS

I f Christ came to the Olympics, He would witness a scene curiously peppered with religious references and gestures. In addition to a subtle, quasi-religious atmosphere generated by various rituals and rhetoric, a hand-painted sign inevitably pops up in the stadium announcing that 'Jesus Saves'. Other signs call attention to Biblical passages such as John 3:16, the apparent favourite of evangelicals: 'God loved the world so much that he gave his only Son, that everyone who has faith in Him may not die but have eternal life.' Another favourite verse for display is the more athletically appropriate Philippians 4:13: 'I have strength for anything through Him who gives me power.'[1]

GOING GOD'S WAY

The impulse to demonstrate one's piety is not confined to the spectators' gallery. Some Olympic athletes dutifully say prayers and make the sign of the cross prior to their events. Emulating the ritual that Carl Lewis performed after each of his four record-breaking events at Los Angeles in 1984, winners frequently drop to a knee with bowed head, folded prayerful hands or an index finger pointing heavenward. The message seems simple and clear: victory comes from God; thanks be to God.

Kurt Angle, an American wrestler, played this game to the hilt. Upon winning a gold medal at the Atlanta Games in 1996, Angle fell to his knees wailing and gushing with gratitude to God while nearly three million television viewers watched the spectacle. He cried throughout the medal-awards ceremony; he cried when he hugged family and friends; he even cried in a subsequent news conference.[2]

As people soon learned, Angle was a 200-pound bundle of pent-up emotions. When he was in high school, his father died. During his college days, a beloved coach was brutally murdered. Then, just a year before the Atlanta Olympics, Angle suffered a severe neck injury that would have prevented a saner man from ever wrestling again. But wrestle he did, with regular shots of

Kurt Angle after winning a
gold medal in wrestling at
the Atlanta Olympics in
1996. (Allsport)

medication and a green light from God: 'I prayed that day [when a doctor advised him never to wrestle again] and God said do it'.[3]

So when the referee raised his hand signalling an Olympic victory, Angle thought it only natural to thank God for strength and protection. 'I knew when my neck was hurt, God was there, watching over me', he later told a reporter. 'I knew when I was wrestling in the Olympic Games that He was watching over me. I knew when I won the gold medal that He intended me to win.'[4]

Surely this mixture of simple faith and superstitious blarney grates on the nerves of any rational listener. Yet Angle saved his trump evangelical card for the end. God wanted him to win, he insisted, because:

> He wanted someone like me to spread the Word and be a role model for kids. I knew that from the beginning. I believe in spreading my word and showing kids they can make their dreams come true and they have to be big believers in God. I feel He's called me to do that. He made me the best in the world so a lot of people would respect me and I could tell them, 'Hey, God's the way to go'.[5]

Just a few years ago, this use of a sports podium to point to God as 'the way to go' would have been dismissed as the tacky rantings of a born-againer, a fundamentalist Protestant. Most critics would probably also assume him to be from the United States, where revivalistic fundamentalism has flourished in various guises for more than a century. Angle broke the stereotype, at least half-way — he is an American, but a Roman Catholic.

Nonetheless, his piety fits comfortably within the evangelical mould, as defined by Wheaton College sociologist James Mathiesen. Evangelicals today are concerned with doctrines such as the inerrancy of scripture, the centrality of Christ's crucifixion and resurrection, and the necessity of a personal 'new birth' experience, says Mathiesen, 'but primarily when those [beliefs] affect their concern with evangelising the world'.[6]

The impulse to 'witness', to spread the word that convinces

don't believe in endorsing my competition', he said soberly. 'I feel very strongly about loyalty to my own company.' As usual, Barkley spoke more colourfully, and to the essence of the issue: 'Us Nike guys are loyal to Nike because they pay us a lot of money. I have two million reasons not to wear Reebok.'[19]

The commercial pettiness of this controversy provoked a *New York Times* journalist to observe that Nike is a Greek word for the goddess of victory, but that Nike could well come to mean 'broken-winged goddess of greed'.[20] Similarly distressed, editors of a liberal weekly, the *Nation,* predicted that Olympic winners would soon be wearing the colours of Froot Loops or Siemens rather than their national colours. 'If there are still gods on Olympus watching these events', the *Nation* concluded in the wake of the 1992 Olympics, 'they must be depressed about the future'.[21]

In the end, both Barkley and Jordan wore Reebok warm-ups in the medal ceremony, but wrapped themselves in the American flag to cover the little company label on their jackets. Another superstar, Michael 'Magic' Johnson, joined them in that gesture, a bizarre but appropriate obscuring of commercial interests under a prime patriotic symbol, all pinned to the altar of sport.[22]

Rumour has it that Christ did not stay around for the medal awards that day. He had seen enough, heard enough, felt enough discomfort. As He left the stadium, He was heard to mutter something about 'graven images' and 'golden calves'.

others to accept Christ, lies at the heart of the evangelical's eagerness to use the Olympic Games as a pulpit for the greater glory of God. Television cameras afford a global audience for gold-winning preachers. As sports literature scholar Jack Higgs reminds us, the Olympics have become a 'prime time for religious proselytism'.[7]

Since 1964 proselytising has gone on at every Olympics, but never on the scale of the 1996 Atlanta Games. In good Bible Belt fashion, Atlanta prides itself on being progressively modern but still supportive of traditional religious institutions, especially the churches engaged in 'outreach' programs of growth. As the Summer Games approached, more than 100,000 local, national and foreign zealots pooled their efforts to run vacation Bible schools, to conduct sports clinics for inner-city youths and to distribute plan-of-salvation tracts at concerts and local ball games as well as at the various Olympic venues. The American Bible Society printed some five million New Testaments for distribution; Southern Baptists prepared one million 'hospitality bags' containing evangelistic messages.[8]

QUIET FIRE

This recent flurry of evangelistic activity has few counterparts prior to the 1960s. Eric Liddell, the subject of the award-winning film, *Chariots of Fire,* seems to be the father of evangelical Olympism. To be sure, Liddell was muscular Christianity incarnate. He blended athletic skill and enthusiasm with religious conviction and fervour in a manner that would make Tom Brown envious.

Born of Scottish missionaries in turn-of-century China, Liddell was sent to school in London where he captained the cricket and rugby teams. He collected an armful of school track records, including 10.2 seconds in the 100-yard dash. Moving on to Edinburgh University, he continued to dominate track events. During his entire undergraduate athletic career, he lost only one race. All the while, his speed worked further to his advantage as an outside winger on the rugby field. In 1921 he won several caps for Scotland in international matches against Wales, England and France. By the end of that year, he was considered indisputably the best athlete in Scotland.[9]

Liddell's fame peaked in the early months of 1922, just as a group of university students launched an interdenominational evangelistic crusade throughout Scotland. Unable to reach hardened people in working-class towns, they turned to Liddell for help. His heroic status, they reasoned, would attract miners and factory operatives. They were right. Reasonably good gatherings turned into large crowds, especially when people learned that Liddell could spin a good homily as well as run a good race.

In truth, Liddell was a shy young man. As an athlete he hated the limelight that required him to talk to reporters and pose for photographs. His 'sermons' featured no wagging of the finger, no thumping of the fist, no prescriptions for his audience. He was confessional, not bombastic. He quietly told listeners what God meant to him; he spoke of the strength and confidence he felt from the sure knowledge of God's loving support, and of his faith in God's authority over all present and future events. As one biographer puts it, Liddell's presentation was 'more of a quiet chat than a sermon'.[10]

It is a message and a style ages removed from the contemporary evangelical tendency to propagate a crass view of the atonement, a simplistic three- or four-step 'plan of salvation', and a marketplace tactic that hawks the Gospel more crudely than when Tetzel sold his indulgences in the sixteenth century. Eric Liddell is scarcely even a distant cousin, much less the father, of the modern evangelical impulse to use sport as a platform to convert the masses.

Thanks to the makers of *Chariots of Fire*, he is best known for his refusal to run a 100-metres preliminary heat on a Sunday at the Paris Olympics in 1924. From his strict Calvinist upbringing, he believed Sunday to be the Christian Sabbath, sacrosanct, reserved for prayer, worship and rest. So while Harold Abrahams ran preliminary heats on his way to winning a gold medal in the 100-meters, Liddell addressed the congregation at the Scots Kirk on the other side of Paris. His principles intact, he was inserted into another event, the 400 metres, and later in the week won his gold medal.

Shortly after the Paris Games, Liddell went off to China to take the missionary mantle from the shoulders of his parents in the land of his birth. Early in World War 2, Japanese troops captured him and other Westerners, placing them in an internment camp. There Liddell conducted sports programs, taught the children science and math, and occasionally led services of worship.

On winter evenings Liddell could be found using old curtains, sheets and towels to repair hockey sticks, tennis rackets and cricket bats in preparation for spring and summer activities. He still refused to take part in Sunday sports, but once when a field hockey match on Sunday afternoon broke out in a fight, he intervened and refereed the game to its end.

Sad to say, Liddell died of a brain tumour just a few months before the war ended. All 1800 people in the camp gathered for an outdoor graveside funeral service. Some were reportedly surprised to hear about his Olympic triumph. They knew him to be an athlete, a kind, intelligent Christian, and a devoted pastor, but not an Olympic champion. If Christ comes to the Olympics, one can only hope that He can find the modest, principled spirit of Eric Liddell amidst the showy physical and verbal antics calculated to sell viewers on the Lord Jesus Christ.

LEAPS OF FAITH

In 1988 an English triple-jumper, Jonathan Edwards, engaged in something of a replay of the Eric Liddell saga, but brought it to an altogether different conclusion. Edwards, the eldest son of an Anglican vicar, mimed Liddell in holding to Sunday as a day reserved for reflection and worship, not work or sport. Edwards'

Eric Liddell, portrayed in the film *Chariots of Fire*, won the 400-metres race at the 1924 Olympics after refusing to run a 100-metres heat on a Sunday because he believed Sunday to be sacrosanct, reserved for prayer, worship and rest. (courtesy of Heather Ingham)

position in 1988 was more remarkable than Liddell's in 1924. Like Liddell, many Christians still struggled with the Sunday question in the l920s, but by the 1980s, Sunday had become so secularised that Edwards stood out like an artifact, if not a sore thumb.

Edwards' conviction came, in part, from his conservative parents, but in larger measure from his own involvement in religious matters. Growing up in the small seaside town of Ilfracombe in southwest England, he regularly studied the Bible at night. His social life largely revolved around church activities. After graduating from Durham University, he got a job in Newcastle and there joined a lively Baptist congregation rather than a more moderate Anglican church.[11]

As the Seoul Olympics approached in 1988, Edwards was considered the second-best triple jumper in the British Isles. He seemed assured of a place on the Olympic team — until the national trials were scheduled for a Sunday. Edwards decided not to compete, and instantly became something of a celebrity. On the morning of the trials, television crews showed up at his church.

Despite his absence from the trials, British officials weighed prior performances and gave Edwards a place on the team. At Seoul the Liddell-like fairy tale collapsed when Edwards failed to qualify for the finals. Four years later, at Barcelona, he was yet again eliminated in preliminary heats.[12]

Edwards' Sunday principle, it seems, had betrayed him athletically. Over the years he repeatedly missed important meetings and training sessions that happened to fall on his 'Christian Sabbath'. In 1991 he even skipped the World Championships in Tokyo because the triple-jump finals were scheduled for Sunday. Finally, in the spring of 1993 he announced a change of mind. His decision, he insisted, was 'very much between my conscience and God'.[13]

Determined still to honour God by becoming the best triple-jumper possible, Edwards practised more regularly, accelerated his weight-lifting program and found new coaches who suggested innovative techniques. In 1995 he competed in fourteen track events, and lost not a single event; he broke the triple-jump world record three times. From the Atlanta Olympics he took home a silver medal.

Edwards' similarities to Eric Liddell were quite coincidental. He did not even see the film *Chariots of Fire* until after his own change of mind, fully a dozen years after the film was released. In fact, he was a bit agitated by the film because it seemed to portray sport as something a Christian should not do on Sunday. 'What I do in sport comes out of my dedication to God', said Edwards. 'Maybe there was a conflict for Liddell; I do not have that conflict.'[14]

Instead of idolising Liddell, Edwards warmed to the film's depiction of Harold Abrahams because Abrahams was 'single-minded, pretty professional' like Edwards himself. In 1994 he made some $100,000 in appearance fees and during the following year (the first year he trained and competed on Sunday), he received an appearance fee of nearly $20,000 per meeting for a total annual income of $400,000.

Fully two decades before Jonathan Edwards' Atlanta coup, another silver medalist took home not only a token of victory but also a seed of faith. The venue was the Montreal Olympics of 1976; the athlete was Nancy Lieberman, a brash teenager, the youngest member of the American women's basketball squad.

Raised in a Jewish home that observed high holidays but otherwise gave little attention to matters of faith, Lieberman by her own admission knew 'next to nothing' about religion. Her roommate in Montreal's Olympic village was Nancy Dunkle, a born-again Christian who frequently read her Bible. 'She'd talk about Jesus and God and I would be like, "Who's Jesus?"' Lieberman recalled years later. In bed each night after the lights were out, Lieberman asked question after question, and Dunkle patiently answered each one as best she could.[15]

This exposure to evangelical Christianity coincided with a profound sense of emptiness felt by young Lieberman. After her team won the silver in the basketball tournament, she went back to her room in the Olympic village, sat on the edge of her bed, and cried. 'I was so empty', she remembered. 'I was happy we won, but it really wasn't fulfilling like I thought it would be ... There was something missing in my life, and I think it was some sort of faith.'

The Hound of Heaven pursued her, it seems, beyond the Olympics and into Old Dominion University, where Lieberman enrolled that fall as a freshman. Soon Old Dominion's men's team was playing a pre-season exhibition game against a touring evangelical God-squad, Athletes in Action. Ralph Drollinger, who had previously played at UCLA, struck up a conversation with Lieberman. Sensing her keen interest, he encouraged her to accept Christ into her life. They prayed together, and Liberman ever afterwards looked on that evening as her moment of spiritual birth.

Given her Jewish heritage and her general ignorance about Christian doctrine, she chose to keep her conversion to herself. Not until 1980 (four years later) did she inform a Dallas sportswriter, who in turn informed the world, that she was a 'born-again Christian'. In truth, she was a most unusual born-again Christian, for she lacked the evangelical zeal to urge others to believe as she believed. 'I don't tell anybody, "You have to be a Christian"', she admits. By the more fundamentalist of evangelical standards, Lieberman is a heretic. 'But whether you're Jewish or Buddhist or Catholic or whatever', she adds, 'I think it's important to have a strong faith in God.' Like English triple-jumper Jonathan Edwards, American basketballer Nancy Lieberman associated the Olympics with a leap of faith.

TIES THAT BIND

Why this cozy connection between modern sport and evangelical piety? The question is not new. As early as 1899, social scientist

Thorstein Veblen said that 'religious zeal' and the 'sporting element' derived from similar sources: the need to distinguish oneself and the urge to believe in divine beneficence or good luck. In the arcane academic terms of his day, Veblen insisted that 'the habitation to sports, perhaps especially to athletic sports, acts to develop the propensities which find satisfaction in devout observances'.[16]

In more decipherable terms, religion and sport interlock because of several common characteristics. The evangelical mindset is particularly akin to athleticism. Structurally, evangelical religious and athletic interests mirror each other, the one finding reinforcement in the other. For one thing, they share a simple, clear-cut vision of reality. For the born-again Christian, one either believes in Christ or rejects Christ; people are either 'saved' or 'lost', bound for heaven or doomed to hell; they are either winners or losers. 'It is a dramatic, stark, even simple faith', says historian Martin Marty. 'There is little toleration for ambiguity, just like in sports. You win or you lose ... Classical Judaism, Catholicism and [mainstream] Protestantism make room for doubt: not evangelical Christianity.'[17]

The born-again athlete is twice blessed with definite rules, boundaries and measures of success. At the Olympics, the evangelical's simple plan of salvation and childlike trust in an infallible Bible are complemented by similarly precise athletic standards. The long jump is measured exactly; the sprint is timed to the millisecond. Even boxing and gymnastics contests are scored with attention to minute details. In the end, an Olympic athlete either wins a medal or goes home empty-handed, saved or damned.

Evangelicalism and athleticism share a clarity of vision that is difficult to find elsewhere amidst the complexities of modern life. As sport writer Leonard Koppett explains, Olympic Games (like all athletic contests) thrive on the illusion that the outcome of a contest really matters. The media, spectators and athletes themselves keep the myth alive: that competitive sport is something

more than big business or nationalistic vanity, that it has something fundamentally to do with the enlargement of the human
spirit. 'Psychologically', says Koppett, 'sports offer an island of
stability in a confusing, shifting cosmos.'[18]

So does evangelical religion. And that is perhaps its strongest
appeal today. Its tenets are definite, not vague; it requires spiritual commitment; and it provides a guidebook for living, the Bible.
In the values game, neither secular hedonism nor flexible, prag-
matic liberalism appeals to the evangelical who attempts to 'follow Christ' in the larger social arena. Like Puritans of old, the
born-again Christian functions best with an orderly set of rules
and firm discipline.

So do athletes. Moreover, piety and sport share a tendency
towards ritual, and sport thrives on it. While the guardians of the
Olympic temple work to perpetuate the rituals surrounding the
opening ceremonies, the awarding of medals and the closing
events, athletes themselves engage in numerous little rituals that
put their mind at ease. They eagerly repeat the sequences and the
mantras that saw them to earlier victories. Edwin Moses, the
gold-medal winner in the 400-metre hurdles at Montreal in 1976
and again at Los Angeles in 1984, always did three hours of
stretches in the same order, at the same pace, to the same music
before each event. Presumably, these rituals prepare athletes to
produce their competitive best.[19]

Rituals frequently steer perilously close to superstition, and all
the more so when sport is involved. In 1972 a leading Australian
racehorse of the day was in Perth training for the Melbourne Cup
when a severe leg injury provoked trainers to consider destroying
the animal. A Perth nun happened to be in France, visiting the
shrine at Lourdes, from whence she sent holy water to rub on the
injured leg. A Catholic writer reasonably wondered if the horse
had taken the place of God for Australians.[20]

No clear line separates religion and superstition in the
Olympic stadium. Athletes, grasping for every advantage they can

find, are notoriously superstitious. Granted, one person's superstition might be another person's religious faith, but surely a prayer for athletic victory is as flagrantly superstitious as is a rabbit's foot or a Papal-blessed medallion. After the event, to thank God publicly for divine assistance in the defeat of an opponent is an insult both to God and to the opponent, whose prayers (if said) presumably were not answered.[21]

The most important connection between born-again religion and modern sport is forged by the consumer culture in whose womb they have both been born and at whose table they feed. Both are 'products' that require distribution; both eagerly advertise and sell their wares. Promotional staffs call it good business. Evangelicals call it 'witnessing' and 'sharing' an entrusted spiritual treasure. 'I knew when I won the gold medal that [God] intended me to win', said wrestler Kurt Angle. 'He wanted someone like me to spread the Word and be a role model for kids.'[22]

Maybe. But if Christ came to the Olympics, we don't know whether He would be embarrassed or delighted at things done and mantras uttered in His name. During a break in the action, He would do well to drop into a nearby secondhand bookshop, find a dusty 1989 copy of *Sports Illustrated*, and read sportswriter Curry Kirkpatick's pertinent reference to German tennis champion Boris Becker as a young man who had not yet burned out from physical stress and fame. Miracle of miracles: Becker refrained from thanking God for 'putting the top-spin on his lob'.[23]

CONCLUDING THE GAMES — FAITH FROM START TO FINISH

T he athletes have finished their athletic endeavours. Bring on the colourful closing ceremonies. Athletes enter the stadium for the last time, now mingling with each other regardless of nationality or athletic specialty. A few are medal winners but all have won something better: new friendships and priceless memories. All are aglow with the sights and sounds of the moment.

This casual, somewhat disorderly stroll at the outset of the closing ceremony originated at the Melbourne Games in 1956, replacing the earlier closing parade of separate squads marching behind their national flags. Apparently the idea originated with a carpenter's apprentice, a Chinese-Australian youth whose family had immigrated to Australia.[1]

At Tokyo eight years later, British journalist Brian Glanville observed that 'the many and various solemnities of the closing ceremony were redeemed by the mass entry of the athletes themselves, who, refusing to take it as anything but a joyous celebration, poured into the stadium' waving their hands, hats and umbrellas. Now free of the pressure to perform, athletes shouted, danced, sang, and clapped. 'It was in vain for a prim young woman to admonish them through the loudspeakers to march in eights', added Glanville. 'Their exuberance was not to be contained even by the most self-conscious of quasi-religious occasions.'[2]

King Festivity reigned, and continues to do so at every closing ceremony. Lively music fills the air; brilliant fireworks light up the sky. Dance and mass exhibitions play on themes of ethnic and racial diversity, and on international brotherhood and goodwill. High above the scene flies the Olympic flag, five interlocked rings set on a plain white background, symbolising the linkage of the five continents in this gathering of competitive but friendly athletes from all over the world. Finally, after a few farewell speeches and the dousing of the Olympic flame, the athletes with their support crews, families and friends return home.

What about Christ? Where does He go from here? Should we not invite Him into our home and community? Could we convince Him to address our government leaders, our various stock exchanges, or at least our councils of churches and synagogues? Now that He has tasted a bit of our sporting enthusiasm, might He even be interested in attending a World Cup fixture, a Grand Final, or a Wimbledon tournament?

No, He will not stay. Consider Albert Schweitzer's summary of the 'curious history' of the study of the life of Jesus:

> It set out in quest of the historical Jesus, believing that when it had found Him it could bring Him straight into our time as a Teacher and Saviour ... But He does not stay; He passes by our time and returns to His own. What surprised and dismayed the theology of the last forty years was that, despite all forced and arbitrary interpretations, it could not keep Him in our time, but had to let him go.[3]

The historian in Schweitzer concluded that the historical Jesus would forever be 'to our time a stranger and an enigma'. For Schweitzer the Christian believer, that was just as well because it was 'not Jesus as historically known, but Jesus as spiritually risen within people, who is significant for our time and can help it'. In summary, 'Not the historical Jesus, but the spirit which goes forth from Him and in the spirits of men strives for new influence and rule, is that which overcomes the world'.[4]

This gold-medal spirit was what inspired the first Christians. For Saul of Tarsus it not only caused a change of name but also a radical change of direction, of associates and of resolve. 'With all these witnesses [spectators] of faith around us like a cloud', the Apostle Paul wrote to the Hebrews, 'we must throw off every encumbrance, every sin to which we cling, and run with resolution the race for which we are entered, our eyes fixed on Jesus, on whom faith depends from start to finish'.[5]

As sport turns to religion for time-honoured rituals and mythologies, religious faith draws upon the metaphorical richness of athleticism. Inspiration flows from the one to the other and back again, especially at the Olympics. Faith, hope and charity are the virtues that make a difference, insisted the early Christians. Olympic enthusiasts agree. For all their petty flaws and garish excesses, the Olympic Games embody a bouyant faith, a hopeful optimism and a charitable ethic that humanity would be the poorer without. Sport as well as religion depends on faith from start to finish.

NOTES

CHAPTER I BRINGING CHRIST TO THE OLYMPICS – AN EXERCISE IN IMAGINATION

1   See Jaroslav Pelikan (1985), *Jesus Through the Centuries: His Place in the History of Culture*, Yale University Press, New Haven, CT.

2   Albert Schweitzer (1960, originally published in German in 1906), *The Quest of the Historical Jesus: A Critical Study of Its Progress from Reimarus to Wrede*, Macmillan, New York, p. 403.

3   James Russell Lowell (1890), 'A Parable', in *The Poetic Works of James Russell Lowell*, vol. 1, Houghton Mifflin, Boston, pp. 267–69.

4   William T. Stead (1964), *If Christ Came to Chicago*, Living Books, New York, pp. 6–7; and Stead (1894), '"If Christ Came to Chicago!" My Book, and Why It Was Written', *Review of Reviews*, vol. 9, May, p. 508.

5   See Joseph O. Baylen (1964), 'A Victorian's "Crusade" in Chicago, 1893–1894', *Journal of American History*, vol. 51, Dec., pp. 418–31.

6   Edward Everett Hale (1894), *If Jesus Came to Boston*, Lawson, Wolfe, & Co., Boston; cf. Francis Nathan Peloubet (c. 1900),*The Loom of Life and If Christ Were a Guest in Our Home*, United Society of Christian Endeavor, Boston.

7   Stead, *If Christ Came to Chicago*, p. 429. See the useful introduction by Harvey Wish in the 1964 edition, pp. 11–17.

8   Charles M. Sheldon (1925), *Charles M. Sheldon: His Life Story*, George H. Horan Company, New York, pp. 10l–107.

9   Bruce Barton (1914), *A Young Man's Jesus*, Pilgrim Press, Boston, pp. 1–8, 14.

10 Quoted in Warren I. Susman (1984), *Culture as History: The Transformation of American Society in the Twentieth Century*, Pantheon, New York, p. 129. For Barton, see pp. 122–31; cf. T.J. Jackson Lears (1983), 'From Salvation to Self-Realization: Advertising and the Theraputic Roots of the Consumer Culture, 1880–1930', in *The Culture of Consumption*, eds Richard Wightman Fox and T.J. Jackson Lears, Pantheon Books, New York, pp. 30–37.

11 See Leo P. Ribuffo (1981), 'Jesus Christ as Business Statesman: Bruce Barton and the Selling of Corporate Capitalism', *American Quarterly*, vol. 33, summer, pp. 206–31; cf. William E. Leuchtenburg (1993),*The Perils of Prosperity, 1914–1932*, University of Chicago Press, Chicago, pp. 188–89.

12 Carlo Levi (1947), *Christ Stopped at Eboli: The Story of a Year*, trans. Frances Frenaye, Farrar, Strauss and Company, New York.

13 Frank McCourt (1996), *Angela's Ashes: A Memoir*, Scribner, New York, pp. 205–206.

14 Schweitzer, *The Quest of the Historical Jesus,* p. 4.
15 Reynolds Price (1999), 'Jesus of Nazareth Then and Now', *Time,* vol. 154, 6 Dec. 1999, p. 88.

CHAPTER 2 GODS AND GAMES — RELIGIOUS ASPECTS OF THE MODERN OLYMPICS

1 Jaroslav Pelikan (1985), *Jesus Through the Centuries: His Place in the History of Culture,* Yale University Press, New Haven, CT, p. 220.
2 See Allen Guttmann (1978), *From Ritual to Record: The Nature of Modern Sport,* Columbia University Press, New York; cf. John Marshall Carter and Arnd Kruger, eds (1990), *Ritual and Record: Sports Records and Quantification in Pre-modern Societies,* Greenwood, Westport, CT.
3 See Luke 9: 10–17.
4 For monographic treatments of the religious basis of sport in antiquity, see A.D. Touney and Steffan Wenig (1971), *Sport in Ancient Egypt,* trans. Joan Becker, Amsterdam Gruner and Ludwig Drees (1968), *Olympia: Gods, Artists and Athletes,* trans. Gerald Onn, Praeger, New York. For a survey summary, see William J. Baker (1996) 'Religion' in *Encyclopedia of World Sport: From Ancient Times to the Present,* 3 vols, eds David Levinson and Karen Christensen, ABC-CLIO, Santa Barbara, CA, vol. 2, pp. 792–99.
5 For the medieval mixture of religion and sport, see Thomas S. Hendricks (1991), *Disputed Pleasures, Sport and Society in Preindustrial England,* Greenwood, Westport, CT, pp. 13–68; and William J. Baker (1988), *Sports in the Western World* University of Illinois Press, Urbana, pp. 42–55.
6 For English Puritans and sport, see Hendricks, *Disputed Pleasures,* pp. 99–127, and Dennis Brailsford (1969), *Sport and Society: Elizabeth to Anne,* Routledge and Kegan Paul, London; for the American story, see Bruce C. Daniels (1995) *Puritans at Play: Leisure and Recreation in Colonial New England,* St Martin's Press, New York, and Nancy L. Struna (1996), *People of Prowess: Sport, Leisure and Labor in Early Anglo-America,* University of Illinois Press, Urbana.
7 From Charles Kingley's *Health and Education* (1874), quoted in Tony Ladd and James A. Mathiesen (1999), *Muscular Christianity: Evangelical Protestants and the Development of American Sport,* Baker Books, Grand Rapids, MI, p. 16.
8 See David Newsome (1961), *Godliness and Good Learning: Four Studies on a Victorian Ideal,* John Murray, London; and J.A. Mangan (1981), *Athleticism is the Victorian and Edwardian Public School: The Emergence and Consolidation of an Educational Ideology,* Cambridge University Press, Cambridge; cf. Bruce Haley (1978), *The Healthy Body and Victorian Culture,* Harvard University Press, Cambridge, MA, and

Kathleen E. McCrone (1988), *Playing the Game: Sport and the Physical Emancipation of English Women, 1870-1914*, University Press of Kentucky, Lexington, KY.

9 For the Hughes-Arnold connection, see Edward C. Mack and W.H.G. Armytage (952), *Thomas Hughes*, Benn, London, pp. 20-25.

10 Allen Guttmann (1992), *The Olympics: A History of the Modern Games*, University of Illinois Press, Urbana, p. 9. For the manner in which Coubertin misread Arnold's religion, see John J. MacAloon (1981), *This Great Symbol: Pierre de Coubertin and the Origins of the Modern Olympic Games*, University of Chicago Press, Chicago, pp. 62-64.

11 Pierre de Coubertin (1967), *The Olympic Idea*, ed. Carl Diem Institut, Verlag Karl Hofmann, Stuttgart, p. 131.

12 But see John Hoberman (1986), *The Olympic Crisis: Sport, Politics and the Moral Order*, Caratzas, New Rochelle, NY, p. 110, for a critical comparison of Comte and Coubertin.

13 Siegfried von Kortzfleisch (1970), 'Religious Olympism', *Social Research: An International Quarterly of Political and Social Science*, vol. 37, p. 234.

14 Hoberman, *The Olympic Crisis*, pp. 38, 41-42; Coubertin, *The Olympic Idea*, p. 118.

15 MacAloon, *This Great Symbol*, pp. 209-15.

16 Guttmann, *This Olympics*, p. 32.

17 Roland Renson (1996), *The Games Reborn: The VIIth Olympiad, Antwerp 1920*, Pandora, Antwerp, p. 30.

18 Ture Widlund (1994), 'Ethelbert Talbot: His Life and Place in Olympic History', *Citius, Altius, Fortius: The International Society of Olympic History Journal*, vol. 2, no. 2, pp. 7-14. For a different slant on the source of the Olympic credo (contending that it came from Coubertin's reading of Ovid), see David C. Young (1994), 'On the Source of the Olympic Credo', *Olympika: The International Journal of Olympic Studies*, vol. 3, pp. 17-25.

19 de Coubertin, *The Olympic Idea*, p. 57.

20 MacAloon, *This Great Symbol*, p. 141; Walter Umminger (1963), *Supermen, Heroes and Gods*, trans. James Clark, Thames & Hudson, pp. 33-34. For a slightly different translation of Coubertin's Berlin speech, see Ove Korsgaard (1990), 'Sport as a Practice of Religion: The Record as Ritual', in Carter and Kruger, *Ritual and Record*, p. 115.

21 Kortsfleisch, 'Religious Olympism', p. 234; Allen Guttmann 1985), 'The Belated Birth and Threatened Death of Fair Play', *The Yale Review*, vol. 74, p. 533.

22 Guttmann, *The Olympics*, p. 83; for Brundage, see Allen Guttmann (1984), *The Games Must Go On: Avery Brundage and the Olympic Movement*, Columbia University Press, New York.

23 For commentary on the religious aspects of the ritual and dogma of the

modern Olympics, see John J. MacAloon (1978), 'Religious Themes and Structures in the Olympic Movement and the Olympic Games', *Philosophy, Theology and History of Sport and Physical Activity*, eds Fernand Landry and William A.R. Orban, Symposia Specialists, Miami, Fl, pp. 161–69.

24 Pierre de Coubertin (1908), 'Why I Revived the Olympic Games', *Fortnightly Review*, vol. 90, July, pp. 110–15.

25 See Thomas Alkemeyer and Alfred Richartz (1993), 'The Olympic Games: From Ceremony to Show', *Olympika: The International Journal of Olympic Studies*, vol. 2, pp. 79–89.

26 John J. MacAloon (1988), 'Double Visions: Olympic Games and American Culture', in *The Olympic Games in Transition*, eds Jeffrey O. Segrave and Donald Chu, Human Kinetics Books, Champaign, IL, p. 285.

CHAPTER 3 GOOD GAMES — AFFIRMING THE ATHLETIC PLEASURES OF THE FLESH

1   For examples see Dick Schaap (1975), *An Illustrated History of the Olympics*, Knopf, New York, pp. 4–5.

2   John A. Lucas (1988), 'A Decalogue of Olympic Games Reform', *The Olympic Games in Transition*, eds Jeffrey O. Segrave and Donald Chu, Human Kinetics Books, Champaign, IL, p. 428.

3   Allen Guttmann (1992), *The Olympics: A History of the Modern Games*, University of Illinois Press, Urbana, p. 17.

4   John J. MacAloon (1981), *This Great Symbol: Pierre de Coubertin and the Origins of the Modern Olympic Games*, University of Chicago Press, Chicago, p. 234.

5   Schaap, *An Illustrated History of the Olympics*, p. 138.

6   Guttmann, *The Olympics*, p. 85.

7   Geoffrey Miller (1979), *Behind the Olympic Rings*, H.O. Zimman, Inc., Lynn, MA, p. 56.

8   Guttman, *The Olympics*, p. 48.

9   Allen Guttmann (1984), *The Games Must Go On: Avery Brundage and the Olympic Movement*, Columbia University Press, New York, p. 198.

10 Miller, *Behind the Olympic Rings*, p. 55.

11 Guttmann, *The Olympics*, pp. 148, 166–67.

12 For the broad outline of this story, see Uriel Simri (1979), *Women at the Olympic Games*, Wingate Institute, Netanya, Israel; and Betty Spears (1976), 'Women in the Olympics: An Unresolved Problem', in *The Modern Olympics*, eds Peter J. Graham and Horst Ueberhorst, Leisure Press, Cornwall, NY.

13 Reet A. Howell (1985), 'Australia's First Female Olympians', in *Sport History: Olympic Scientific Congress 1984 Official Report*, eds Norbert Mueller and Joachim K. Ruehl, Schors-Verlag, Niedernhausen, pp. 17–29;

and Dennis Phillips (1990), 'Australian Women at the Olympics: Achievement and Alienation', *Sporting Traditions: Journal of the Australian Society for Sports History*, vol. 6, no. 2, May, pp. 184–86.

14 Joan S. Hult (1984), 'American Sportswomen: "Go for the Gold" — 1912–1936', in *Olympic Scientific Congress 1984 Official Report*, pp. 30–43.

15 Phillips, 'Australian Women at the Olympics', p. 185; and Howell, 'Australia's First Female Olympians', pp. 19–20.

16 Allen Guttmann (1991), *Women's Sports: A History*, Columbia University Press, New York, pp. 166–68.

17 Guttmann, *The Olympics*, p. 47.

18 See Doris H. Pieroth (1996), *Their Day in the Sun: Women of the 1932 Olympics*, University of Washington Press, Seattle.

19 Harry Gordon (1994), *Australia and the Olympic Games*, University of Queensland Press, St Lucia, pp. 203–25.

20 Guttmann, *Women's Sports*, pp. 243–45.

21 Gina Daddario (1998), *Women's Sport and Spectacle: Gendered Television Coverage and the Olympic Games*, Praeger, Westport, CT, p. 145; *New York Times*, 23 June 1996.

22 William J. Baker (1987), 'Political Games: The Meaning of International Sport for Independent Africa', in *Sport in Africa: Essays in Social History*, eds William J. Baker and James A. Mangan, Africana Publishing Company, New York, pp. 275, 280–81.

23 *New York Times*, 6 August 1996.

24 See Colin Tatz (1987), *Aborigines in Sport*, Australian Society for Sports History, Adelaide, and Brian Stoddart (1986), *Saturday Afternoon Fever: Sport in the Australian Culture*, Angus & Robertson, Sydney, pp. 158–71.

25 See Baker (1987), 'Political Games', pp. 272–94.

26 Robert Archer and Antoine Bouillon (1982), *The South African Game: Sport and Racism*, Zed Press, London.

27 See Adrian Guelke (1993), 'Sport and the End of Apartheid', in *The Changing Politics of Sport*, ed. Lincoln Allison, Manchester University Press, Manchester, pp. 151–70.

CHAPTER 4 THE POWERS AND THE GLORY — GOING FOR GOLD AND OTHER FALSE GODS

1 William T. Stead (1964), *If Christ Came to Chicago*, Living Books, Chicago, p. 74.

2 Pierre de Coubertin (1988), 'Why I Revived the Olympic Games', in *The Olympic Games in Transition*, eds Jeffrey O. Segrave and Donald Chu, Human Kinetics Books, Champaign, IL, p. 103.

3 See Mandell, Richard D. (1984), *Sport: A Cultural History*, Columbia University Press, New York, pp. 206–207.

4   Allen Guttmann (1984), *The Games Must Go On: Avery Brundage and the Olympic Movement*, Columbia University Press, New York, p. 213.
5   Richard Gruneau and Hart Cantelon (1988), 'Capitalism, Commercialism and the Olympics', in Jeffrey O. Segrave and Donald Chu, p. 347. For some specific examples of athletes capitalising on their gold-medal performances, see Alfred Erich Senn (1999), *Power, Politics and the Olympic Games*, Human Kinetics, Champaign, IL, pp. 259–60.
6   Senn, *Power, Politics and the Olympic Games*, pp. 18, 208; Jennings, Andrew (1996), *The New Lords of the Ring: Olympic Corruption and How to Buy Gold Medals*, Simon & Schuster, London, pp. 43–46.
7   Allen Guttmann (1992), *The Olympics: A History of the Modern Games*, Columbia University Press, New York, p. 160. For Ueberroth's version of this event, see Peter Uberrroth with Richard Levin and Amy Quinn (1985), *Made in America: His Own Story*, William Morrow, New York.
8   Guttmann, *The Olympics*, p. 128.
9   John J. MacAloon (1981), *This Great Symbol: Pierre de Coubertin and the Origins of the Modern Olympic Games*, University of Chicago Press, Chicago, pp. 141–42.
10 MacAloon, *This Great Symbol*, pp. 258–59; cf. pp. 111–12.
11 Pierre de Coubertin (1967, originally published in 1966 in French), *The Olympic Idea: Discourses and Essays*, ed. Carl-Diem Institute, trans. John G. Dixon, Olympischer Sport-Verlag, Stuttgart, p. 3.
12 Mark Dyreson (1998), *Making the American Dream: Sport Culture, and the Olympic Experience*, University of Illinois Press, Urbana, pp. 136–37.
13 Paul Tillich (1948), *The Shaking of the Foundations*, Scribner's, New York, p. 6.
14 Ross Terrill (1987), *The Australians*, Simon & Schuster, New York, p. 71.
15 Ibid.
16 *Sydney Morning Herald*, 8 Sept. 1999.
17 See Richard Cashman's comparison of the Olympics with soccer, its prime competitor for international popularity: 'The Greatest Peacetime Event', in *Staging the Olympics: The Event and Its Impact*, eds Richard Cashman and Anthony Hughes (1999), UNSW Press, Sydney, pp. 4–5.
18 Jack McCallum (1992), 'USA Inc.', *Sports Illustrated*, vol. 77, July 22, pp. 124–26.
19 Harvey Araton (1992), 'I Pledge Allegiance to the Flag Apparel', and Dave Anderson (1992), 'On Loyalty to Company, or Country?' *New York Times*, Aug. 2.
20 Ibid.
21 Anderson, 'On Loyalty to Company'; 'Olympian Greed', *The Nation*, vol. 255, 31 Aug.–7 Sept. 1992, pp. 195–96.
22 Jack McCallum (1992), 'Dreamy', *Sports Illustrated*, vol. 77, 17 Aug. 1992.

CHAPTER 5 PRIME TIME PROSELYTES — EVANGELICALS AT THE OLYMPICS

1 *The New English Bible* (1970) translation.
2 This episode is largely taken from Steve Hubbard (1998), *Faith in Sports: Athletes and Their Religion on and off the Field*, Doubleday, New York, pp. 143–47, 204–205, and Rick Reilly (1996), 'Holding Their Own', *Sports Illustrated*, vol. 85, 12 Aug., pp. 78–83.
3 Hubbard, *Faith in Sports*, p. 145.
4 Ibid.
5 Ibid.
6 Tony Ladd and James A. Mathiesen (1999), *Muscular Christianity: Evangelical Protestants and the Development of American Sport*, Baker Book House, Grand Rapids, MI, p. 214.
7 Robert J. Higgs (1995), *God in the Stadium: Sports and Religion in America*, University Press of Kentucky, Lexington, p. 326.
8 Hubbard, *Faith in Sports*, pp. 44–45. For a momentary ban on the hawking of Jesus in Atlanta's Olympic Park, see pp. 59–60.
9 Catherine Swift (1990), *Eric Liddell*, Bethany House, Minneapolis, pp. 55, 63, 68.
10 Swift, *Eric Liddell*, pp. 78–79.
11 These details are largely taken from Tim Layden (1996), 'Leap of Faith', *Sports Illustrated*, vol. 84, 13 May, pp. 88–97; and Hubbard, *Faith in Sports*, pp. 55–56.
12 Actually, Eric Liddell himself merely won a bronze medal (third place) in one of the *two* events he entered after refusing to run the 100 metres on Sunday. His victory in the 400 metres, dramatised so well in *Chariots of Fire*, overshadowed his poorer performance in the 200 metres (see Swift, *Eric Liddell*, p. 99).
13 Layden, 'Leap of Faith', p. 93.
14 Ibid.
15 For this account of Lieberman's story, see Hubbard, *Faith in Sport*, pp. 130–33.
16 Thorstein Veblen (1953, originally published in 1899), *The Theory of the Leisure Class: An Economic Study of Institutions*, New York, New American Library, pp. 195–97.
17 Quoted in Linda Kay (1982), 'When Christianity Goes Into the Locker Room', *Chicago Tribune*, 17 October.
18 Leonard Koppett (1994), *Sports Illusion, Sports Reality: A Reporter's View of Sports, Journalism and Society*, University of Illinois Press, Urbana, p. 21. Pierre de Coubertin envisaged the modern Olympics as something 'to hold on to' for people who felt 'the ground trembling continually under their feet' (see John J. MacAloon (1981), *This Great*

Symbol: Pierre de Coubertin and the Origins of the Modern Olympic Games, University of Chicago Press, Chicago, p. 188).

19 See Mari Womack (1979), 'Why Athletes Need Ritual: A Study of Magic Among Professional Athletes', in *Sport and the Humanities: A Collection of Original Essays*, ed. W.J. Morgan, University of Tennessee Press, Knoxville, pp. 27–38.

20 Keith Dunstan (1973), *Sports*, Sun Books, Melbourne, pp. 25, 41.

21 On the relation of religion to superstition in athletes, see Eldon E. Snyder and Eldon A. Spreitzer (1983), *Social Aspects of Sport*, Prentice-Hall, Englewood Cliffs, NJ, pp. 272–75.

22 Hubbard, *Faith in Sports*, p. 147.

23 Curry Kirkpatrick (1989), 'Boom Boom', *Sports Illustrated*, vol. 71, 18 Sept., p. 24.

CHAPTER 6 CONCLUDING THE GAMES — FAITH FROM START TO FINISH

1 Harry Gordon (1994), *Australia and the Olympic Games*, University of Queensland Press, Brisbane, pp. 224–24.

2 Brian Glanville (1968), *People in Sport*, Sportsmans Book Club, London, p. 70. For a more negative account of this event in which athletes reportedly engaged in parodic mime, 'pretending to pray before the Emperor who has ceased to be God', see Paul Werrie's comments as translated in John Hoberman (1981), *The Olympic Crisis: Sport, Politics and the Moral Order*, Caratzas, New Rochelle, NY, pp. 99–100.

3 Albert Schweitzer (1960, originally published in German in 1906), *The Quest of the Historical Jesus: A Critical Study of Its Progress from Reimarus to Wrede*, Macmillan, New York, p. 399.

4 Ibid., pp. 399, 40l.

5 Hebrews 12:1–2 (*New English Bible*).

INDEX

Page numbers in *italics* refer to photographs.

teams proudly enter the stadium in the opening ceremonies. Like George Foreman in 1968 and Carl Lewis in 1984, boxers and track athletes dance about waving little flags in celebration of victory. Teams mingle and fraternise in the Olympic village and during the final ceremonies. Similarly benign and memorable, the victor's stand is sprinkled repeatedly with the joyous tears of young men and women for whom the sight of their flag and the sound of their national anthem pack a lethal punch.

Patriotism sometimes turns mean, of course. Age-old antagonisms get played out on the Olympic stage. Only a short step separates the patriot happily honouring his or her own flag from the hostile nationalist waving his or her flag in the face of others. An incident in the London Olympics of 1908 symbolised more than a century of Anglo-American distrust. American athletes, thinking themselves abused and cheated by British officials, refused to lower the Stars and Stripes as they marched past the royal box. Thus was formed a motto that persists to the present: 'This flag dips to no earthly king'.[12]

Nor does the flag dip to any heavenly king. In truth, it dips only to itself in a god-like claim to the hearts and minds of its citizenry, especially as seen in the wake of World War 2, when global events turned the Olympics into a virtual battleground. At the Helsinki Games in 1952, a Soviet team competed for the first time, and for the next four decades Cold War politics pitted the Soviets and their Communist friends against the Western democracies.

More subtly, divided nations, racism and poverty, and the decolonising emergence of new African and Asian nations made for explosive possibilities. Avery Brundage frequently insisted that the Olympic Games were 'contests between individuals and not between nations', and that politics had 'nothing to do with sport', but bans, boycotts, demonstrations and politically motivated violence such as the Palestinian massacre of Israeli athletes at Munich in 1972 regularly appear in the recent history of the Olympics.

Nationalism is like the Hydra of old. You lop off one of its heads and another sprouts immediately. The question for future Olympics is not so much whether or not nationalism will be present, but rather what form it will take.

Christ would most surely recognise it for what it is: a false god that wraps patriotic symbols, rituals and mythologies around athletic events, forever seeking true believers who will be both ideologically and emotionally committed to the nation state.

AT THE ALTAR OF SPORT

Sport itself links up with patriotism and commercialism to constitute a kind of modern trinity. This idolatrous threesome thrives at the Olympics, inspiring commitments and stirring passions that have traditionally been directed towards God.

Protestant theologian Paul Tillich provides a pertinent, helpful definition of religion. One's 'ultimate concern,' says Tillich, is one's religion. It is 'a concern which qualifies all other concerns as preliminary and which itself contains the answer to the question of meaning and of our life'. To what is the bulk of your time, money, energy and devotion given? That is your religion, and therein resides your god.[13]

Of all the great would-be religions in the modern world, sport sits enthroned as a focus of extravagant popular, economic and political attention. Compare the sports page to the religious section of any mass-market newspaper. The former is massive, the latter miniscule. A comparison of sporting crowds and church goers around the world suggests similar disparities in size, not to mention contrasting levels of enthusiasm.

These divergent impressions are especially apparent in Australia, where climate and urban life conspire with egalitarian and anti-puritan attitudes to make competitive, spectator sport supremely important. An expatriate, Ross Terrill, reasons that formal religion 'withered' early in Australian history, so the prime god of Australia became Nature. The great Australian festival, says Terrill, honoured 'outdoor physical struggle' such as war (Anzac Day), efforts to squeeze a living from inhospitable soil (the Royal Agricultural Show), and open-air sports contests (such as the Melbourne Cup and the Grand Finals of Australian Rules Football).[14]

Terrill, a native Victorian, vividly describes the religious patina on a 'great Australian ritual', a cricket test match at the Melbourne Cricket Ground. The ground itself is in the heart of the city, similar to a cathedral site in medieval cities. Some 80,000 people 'hunch on benches as at church', raptly attentive. They politely applaud a fine bowler or batsman, and occasionally register raucous disapproval of an umpire's call. 'Yet tension and reverence fill the stadium as the game goes on for four days, six hours a day. This is Melbourne with its mind on the job; this is Melbourne at worship.' Terrill concludes: 'These pagans have found a God.'[15]

Sydney 'pagans', too, have found the great god Sport, but display as much irreverence towards it as they do towards the usual Heavenly Team. In 1999, on the eve of these New College lectures, the *Sydney Morning Herald* mischievously invited 'poems' beginning with the words, 'If Christ Came to the Sydney Olympics'. For two days light-hearted verses, limericks and pieces of doggerel headed the 'Stay in Touch' section of the *Herald*. My favourite was by Chris Barnes of Ashfield:

If Christ Came to the Sydney Olympics
Would we have cause to cheer?
Would he preach God's Word, and heal the sick
Or just sit back with a beer?
Perhaps he'd even raise those who'd died
But I fear the news report
'Today, Jesus Christ was crucified
For distracting us from sport'.[16]

Arguably, of all the altars to international sport, the Olympics overshadow the World Cup, Wimbledon and all the other claimants to international dominance. At the Barcelona Games in 1992, the false gods of sport, commercialism and patriotism cohered in a unique, pithy fashion. For the first time ever, professional basketball players were allowed to compete in the Olympics. The American squad was a much publicised 'Dream Team' composed mostly of NBA stars — millionaires all.[17]

The gods of corporate America had a field day. Some forty major American corporations — including McDonald's, Nike, Kraft Food, Kellogg's, AT&T and Coca Cola — paid $40 million to be associated with these athletic celebrities in a patriotic effort whose success was never in doubt. *Sports Illustrated* offered a free video of the 'NBA Dream Team' with each new subscription. Entrepreneurs made and sold millions of pins, decals, posters, buttons, pennants, caps, shorts, jerseys, T-shirts and travel bags. A Chicago promoter rightly called the flurry on the road to Barcelona 'the biggest, most expensive marketing deal in the history of sports'.[18]

The Barcelona Games threatened also to be the most contentious. In a re-enactment of the old Greek mythologies that pitted the gods at war against each other, corporations squared off against corporations, contesting for maximum visibility. Athletes with million-dollar endorsement contracts were caught in the bind. Michael Jordan, for example, balked at the marketing of his image and name on T-shirts not made by his own patron, Nike. While Jordan's lawyers negotiated that issue, Reebok caused yet another conflict when it paid a huge sum of money to the United States Olympic committee for the exclusive right to outfit all American athletes in Reebok warm-ups for the medal awards ceremonies.

Fully half of the basketball squad were under contract to Nike, Reebok's prime competitor, but only Jordan and Charles Barkley voiced their dilemma. Jordan had a belief system to maintain. 'I